Multichannel Retailing: A Review and Research Agenda

Other titles in Foundations and Trends® in Marketing

Modeling Dynamic Relations Among Marketing and Performance Metrics
Koen H. Pauwels
ISBN:978-1-68083-490-1

Sales Force Compensation: Trends and Research Opportunities
Dominique Rouziès and Vincent Onyemah
ISBN: 978-1-68083-488-8

From Doubt to Functionality: An Imagery Story
Rashmi Adaval
ISBN:978-1-68083-458-1

Consumer Informational Privacy
Frank T. Beke, Felix Eggers and Peter C. Verhoef
ISBN: 978-1-68083-168-9

Multichannel Retailing: A Review and Research Agenda

Huan Liu
Ph.D. Candidate, University of Groningen,
Faculty of Economics and Business,
Department of Marketing, Nettelbosje 2, 9747 AE Groningen,
The Netherlands, huan.liu@rug.nl &
University of Chinese Academy of Sciences, China

Lara Lobschat
Assistant Professor of Marketing, University of Groningen,
Faculty of Economics and Business, Department of Marketing,
Nettelbosje 2, 9747 AE Groningen, The Netherlands,
l.lobschat@rug.nl

Peter C. Verhoef
Professor of Marketing, University of Groningen,
Faculty of Economics and Business, Department of Marketing,
Nettelbosje 2, 9747 AE Groningen, The Netherlands,
p.c.verhoef@rug.nl

the essence of knowledge

Boston — Delft

Foundations and Trends® in Marketing

Published, sold and distributed by:
now Publishers Inc.
PO Box 1024
Hanover, MA 02339
United States
Tel. +1-781-985-4510
www.nowpublishers.com
sales@nowpublishers.com

Outside North America:
now Publishers Inc.
PO Box 179
2600 AD Delft
The Netherlands
Tel. +31-6-51115274

The preferred citation for this publication is

H. Liu, L. Lobschat and P. C. Verhoef. *Multichannel Retailing: A Review and Research Agenda*. Foundations and Trends® in Marketing, vol. 12, no. 1, pp. 1–79, 2018.

ISBN: 978-1-68083-494-9
© 2018 H. Liu, L. Lobschat and P. C. Verhoef

Foundations and Trends® in Marketing
Volume 12, Issue 1, 2018
Editorial Board

Editorial Scope

Topics

Foundations and Trends® in Marketing publishes survey and tutorial articles in the following topics:

- B2B Marketing
- Bayesian Models
- Behavioral Decision Making
- Branding and Brand Equity
- Channel Management
- Choice Modeling
- Comparative Market Structure
- Competitive Marketing Strategy
- Conjoint Analysis
- Customer Equity
- Customer Relationship Management
- Game Theoretic Models
- Group Choice and Negotiation
- Discrete Choice Models
- Individual Decision Making
- Marketing Decisions Models
- Market Forecasting
- Marketing Information Systems
- Market Response Models
- Market Segmentation
- Market Share Analysis
- Multi-channel Marketing
- New Product Diffusion
- Pricing Models
- Product Development
- Product Innovation
- Sales Forecasting
- Sales Force Management
- Sales Promotion
- Services Marketing
- Stochastic Model

Information for Librarians

Foundations and Trends® in Marketing, 2018, Volume 12, 4 issues. ISSN paper version 1555-0753. ISSN online version 1555-0761. Also available as a combined paper and online subscription.

Contents

Multichannel Retailing: A Review and Research Agenda

Huan Liu[1], Lara Lobschat[2] and Peter C. Verhoef[3]

[1] *University of Groningen, The Netherlands & University of Chinese Academy of Sciences, China; huan.liu@rug.nl*
[2] *University of Groningen, The Netherlands; l.lobschat@rug.nl*
[3] *University of Groningen, The Netherlands; p.c.verhoef@rug.nl*

ABSTRACT

The emergence of multiple channels is reshaping consumers' purchase behavior and retailers' marketing styles. We synthesize existing research on multichannel retailing based on more than 150 articles published in peer-reviewed marketing journals, most after 2006. From this synthesis, we reveal conditions under which both consumers and retailers can benefit from a multichannel context. More specifically, we identify multichannel retailing as a win-win game contingent on market environments, retailer characteristics, channel attributes, product categories, social and situational factors, and customer heterogeneity. Last, we highlight multiple directions for future research.

Keywords: multichannel retailing; multichannel shopping; multichannel marketing.

© Huan Liu, Lara Lobschat and Peter C. Verhoef (2018), "Multichannel Retailing: A Review and Research Agenda", Foundations and Trends® in Marketing: Vol. 12, No. 1, pp 1–79. DOI: 10.1561/1700000059.

1

Introduction

The plethora of new channels has changed the infrastructure of today's retailing environment (Neslin *et al.*, 2006). Especially Internet-based channels (i.e., online and mobile channels) and advanced technologies have created new and innovative opportunities for retailers' marketing activities and improved the flexibility of their marketing decisions (Verhoef *et al.*, 2015). For example, channels such as e-mail, websites, mobile devices, and social media allow retailers to reach consumers through various formats without the limitations of time and location. Technologies such as location-based services installed in mobile phones allow retailers to use the exact locations where target consumers are to transmit coupons and advertisements to them in real time (Andrews *et al.*, 2016; Verhoef *et al.*, 2017). Retailers no longer rely solely on traditional channels (e.g., physical stores, catalogs) given the omnipresence of advanced channels. A report by Episerver (2015) indicates that nearly 95% of retailers realize the importance of a multichannel strategy to target consumers. Another study by Pew Research Center shows that approximately 86% of apparel retailers have already adopted up to four social media channels to communicate with consumers (Morrison, 2015).

A wealth of related research has emerged since the appearance of Internet-based channels. A majority of early studies focused on the intention of consumers to purchase from a retailer's new channels. Later studies have discussed how new channels and the mix of traditional and new channels influence customer loyalty and retailer performance. Some of these studies show that adding a new channel has a positive effect on customer loyalty and firm value by increasing customer revenue, decreasing search cost, and providing better service outcomes to consumers (e.g., Homburg *et al.*, 2014; Wallace *et al.*, 2004). Other studies argue that cannibalization effects exist across channels (e.g., Falk *et al.*, 2007). For example, Ofek *et al.* (2011) show that the addition of a website decreases a retailer's overall profit when competition is intense, because the retailer needs to invest more in customer assistance provided in stores (e.g., greater shelf display, more qualified sales staff, floor samples) to improve differentiation from rivals that do not provide similar store assistance. However, not all customers benefit from the focal retailer's improved store assistance. Huang *et al.* (2016) find that a small percentage of website purchases shifted to a newly added mobile app because of its greater convenience. Other research further indicates that synergy and cannibalization effects co-exist and are contingent on retailer characteristics (e.g., the presence of stores) (Wang and Goldfarb, 2017). In essence, different findings appear in articles on multichannel retailing with different contexts, though little is known about what drives these divergent findings.

Thus, the aim of this article is to present an overview of and draw conclusions from extant studies related to multichannel retailing. Neslin *et al.* (2006) provide an influential review on multichannel retailing that includes both traditional and online channels. Thereafter, academic interest increased dramatically, with a large number of new articles being published on this topic (see Figure 1.1). For example, retailers have adopted additional new channels and new channel technologies with unique characteristics, which has further increased the complexity of multichannel retailing. These new channels generate different effects on retailer performance from the effects of offline and online channels (Fong *et al.*, 2015). Thus, an updated understanding of how retailers and consumers influence and interact with each other in multichannel

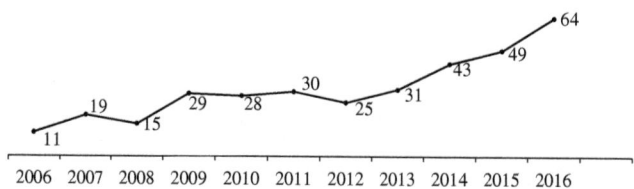

Figure 1.1: The number of published articles on multichannel retailing from 2006.

Notes: We used 14 keywords to search 649 articles from Web of Science, limited to 26 journals of business, economic, management, and psychology, such as *Marketing Science* and *Journal of Retailing*. Reading the abstract of all articles, we deleted those that had low relativity with multichannel retailing. The final number of articles counted in the figure is 345, including one article published in 2017. The 14 keywords are "multichannel retailing," "online offline," "multichannel marketing," "cross-channel," "multichannel marketing," "channel elimination," "channel migration," "channel integration," "multichannel shoppers," "multichannel customers," "multichannel customer management," "mobile marketing," "mobile app," and "purchase journey."

retail contexts is required. More specifically, we focus on the following questions: (1) What factors influence channel choices of retailers and customers? (2) How do retailers employ multichannel marketing strategies, and how do customers use different channels to search and purchase during their purchase journey? and (3) How do multichannel strategies and channel selection behavior affect customer outcomes (e.g., satisfaction, loyalty) and retailer performance (e.g., purchase frequencies, sales, profit)?

After presenting the definitions of key terms used in multichannel retailing, we introduce our framework. Next, we synthesize existing research and specify the three research questions with six subtopics by considering the perspectives of both customers and retailers. At the end of each subtopic, we discuss future research directions derived from research gaps, unresolved issues in practice, and environment changes. We conclude with thoughts about future retailing.

2

Definitions

2.1 Channel

Neslin *et al.* (2006, p. 96) conceptualize a *channel* as "a customer contact point, or a medium through which the firm and the customer interact." To explain the differences across channels, we categorize them into four groups according to their corresponding technologies and functions: (1) offline channels, mainly including physical stores and catalogs; (2) online channels, including e-mail and websites; (3) mobile channels, including mobile websites and apps; and (4) other touchpoints,[1] such as social media, word of mouth, advertising, promotions, and thank-you cards. The major difference between the first three categories is the technology used (i.e., without Internet, with Internet, and with mobile Internet). The difference between the first three categories and the last one involves channel functions. In most cases, the former have both informational and transactional functions, while the latter emphasizes

---

[1]Verhoef *et al.* (2015, p. 175) define touchpoints as "episodes of direct or indirect contact with a brand or firm." According to this definition, the first three groups of channels are included in touchpoints. Here with "other touchpoints," we mean other touchpoints that cannot be covered in the first three groups of channels.

the informational function and the interaction between customers and retailers.

This article focuses on transactional channels. Of the four channel categories, the most common transactional channels are offline, online, and mobile. In terms of touchpoints (i.e., different social media platforms), some also have transactional functions. However, customers are not yet ready to purchase products directly through social media; they are using such channels to inspire purchases by viewing products and communicating with retailers and friends (Chahal, 2016). Thus, we treat social media as search and communication channels instead of transactional channels. Furthermore, we define our research scope as multichannel retailing, focusing on retail channels instead of omnichannel retailing because omnichannel retailing is discussed as an evolution of multichannel retailing taking a broader perspective of channels including and emphasizing multiple interaction touchpoints (Verhoef *et al.*, 2015).

2.2   Multichannel retailing

Previous studies define multichannel retailing as a set of activities through which retailers sell products or services via more than one channel (Levy and Weitz, 2009; Lin, 2012). In this article, we extend multichannel retailing to a broader concept, including not only retailers' activities but also customers' shopping behavior in a multichannel environment.

2.3   Multichannel marketing

From a retailers' perspective, multichannel marketing is defined as, that retailers provide customers with information, products, services and support through two or more synchronized channels at the same time (Rangaswamy and Van Bruggen, 2005). For example, retailers can develop various marketing strategies on whether to add or eliminate a channel, offer a specific marketing mix across channels, or integrate channels.

2.4 Multichannel customer management

Neslin *et al.* (2006, p. 96) propose the concept of multichannel customer management and define it as "the design, deployment, coordination, and evaluation of channels to enhance customer value through effective customer acquisition, retention and development." The concept is used for guiding retailers to develop multichannel marketing strategies from a customer-centric view.

2.5 Multichannel shopping

From a customers' perspective, we define multichannel shopping as consumers' usage of more than one channel in the shopping process covering different stages (e.g., searching information, purchasing products/ services, obtaining after-sales services). Accordingly, a multichannel shopper is a person who shops in (uses) more than one channel during the buying process (Konuş *et al.*, 2008; Schröder and Zaharia, 2008).

3

Framework

Previous works discuss multichannel customer management from aspects of channel selection, multichannel strategy implementation, and channel evaluation (Neslin *et al.*, 2006; Neslin and Shankar, 2009; Verhoef, 2012), and from the view of how retailers communicate with customers based on customer needs (Kumar, 2010). We propose a framework grounded on these studies and refined by considering the whole interaction decision process between retailers and customers from channel selection to its consequences in retailing contexts. The current framework is served to understand customers' channel choices and responses to retailers' multichannel marketing activities, and help retailers to make better multichannel strategies and resource allocation. Specifically, our framework includes three stages (i.e., input, process, and output stages) (see Figure 3.1) to guide the following discussion. In the input stage, we summarize determinants of channel choice. Retailers decide whether to add or eliminate channels in their channel mix (Konuş *et al.*, 2014; Verhoef, 2012), while consumers decide whether to adopt new channels or migrate from one channel to another. In the process stage, we explain how customers' shopping behavior evolves and how retailers implement marketing strategies in a multichannel environment. Multichannel

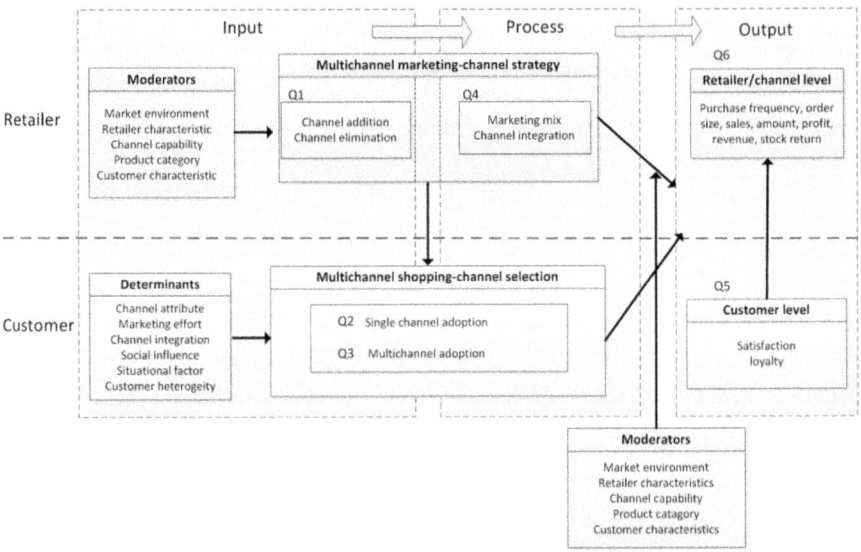

Figure 3.1: A framework for the multichannel retailing literature review.

retailers may implement various marketing-mix and channel integration strategies to attract and retain customers and increase sales. Customers may use different channels to search and purchase in various contexts. In the output stage, we synthesize the consequences of the multichannel activities on both customers and retailers. A retailer's marketing strategies and consumers' shopping behavior across channels affect (1) consumers' satisfaction, retention, and loyalty (Wallace *et al.*, 2004) and (2) retailer and channel performance (e.g., purchase frequencies, sales, profits) (Wang *et al.*, 2015). Note that customer outcomes such as satisfaction and loyalty also affect retailer performance. We also consider several moderators categorized as market-, retailer-, product-, customer-, and context-related (Konuş *et al.*, 2008; Pauwels *et al.*, 2011).

4

RQ1: Determinants of retailers' channel choices

Changing the retail channel mix is an important strategy to improve customer loyalty and experience, increase sales and profits, and respond to competitors' activities (for reviews, see Lewis *et al.*, 2014; Zhang *et al.*, 2010). In this section, we discuss what drives retailers to change their channel mix and add or eliminate channels. One major challenge in answering this question is that very limited research on drivers of retailers' channel choices exists. One exception is the study of Jindal *et al.* (2007), who consider the role of generic firm strategies (i.e., cost-leadership and differentiation) and the impact of customer orientation. They argue that generic strategies affect the breadth of retailers' channel mix because of different strategic natures. They find that retailers with a low-cost strategy use many channels to achieve economies of scale by providing more access to products and services, while those implementing a differentiation strategy also use many channels but keep low intensity in each. Jindal *et al.* maintain that retailers with a strong customer focus aim to deliver an improved customer experience and therefore use a more narrow variety of channels to avoid intra-brand competition and channel conflicts.

To derive more insights, we consider which factors moderate the success of retailers' channel-mix decisions. Extant research suggests the success of a channel decision depends on market environments, retailer characteristics, channel capabilities, product categories, and customer characteristics.

4.1   Market environments

Literature has considered multiple market environment characteristics that are relevant for a retailer's channel choice. Studies find that the addition of a new channel creates more value in a turbulent market characterized by high customer demand volatility, by allowing the firm to spread risk across more channels (Homburg *et al.*, 2014), but do not provide support for the effect of demand growth (Geyskens *et al.*, 2002). Homburg *et al.* (2014) also indicate that adding an online channel is a viable way to differentiate from competitors without online channels, thus generating more value in heavily competitive markets. However, Ofek *et al.* (2011) argue that for apparel and jewelry retailers that sell products with high "touch and feel" attributes, adding an online channel in a market with strong competition does not necessarily yield competitive advantages and profits. This is because, on one side, retailers face higher return costs on websites than offline channels and, on the other side, need to invest more in offline channels to differentiate them from others.

Competitors' marketing activities also matter. Van Nierop *et al.* (2011) find that a competitor's strategies of both introducing a web store and advertising new loyalty programs have negative effects on the value creation of a focal retailer's online channel addition. In summary, extant research suggests that retailers should add channels in turbulent markets, while there is some mixed evidence on the role of competitive intensity. Still, competitor actions may drive changes in the channel mix (Verhoef, 2012).

4.2   Retailer characteristics

Retailer-specific characteristics, including market position, the channel power over distributors, retailer size, sales growth, operating efficiency, and operation experience of different channels, also affect the value creation of channel addition. Homburg *et al.* (2014) find that operating efficiency and achieved sales growth negatively affect the value creation of an online channel addition. This is because the new channel not only is unnecessary for the retailer with high efficiency and sales growth but also needs extra investments and costs of setting up new resources or integrating with existing channels. Geyskens *et al.* (2002) show that the number of established direct channels also has a negative effect on value creation of online channel additions. The more direct channels a retailer already offers, the lower is the likelihood that a new online channel will be perceived as distinct and attract new demand. Channel power is positively related to performance potential of channel additions, because sufficient channel power reduces conflicts with existing channel partners. However, market position (i.e., market leaders vs. market followers) and firm size do not have significant impacts in the two studies.

Findings from the literature indicate that a retailer's channel-introduction strategy also matters in retailers' channel choices. Pauwels and Neslin (2015) explore the value of adding physical stores to a retail website and show differential effects from studies that explore the effects of adding a retail website to a set of existing physical stores (Homburg *et al.*, 2014). In particular, they find that announcing the availability of a new channel can develop customer awareness of this channel and thus enhance value creation. Retailers that are early followers with their channel addition also benefit more from the online channel addition than those that are pioneers and later entrants (Geyskens *et al.*, 2002). Jindal *et al.* (2007) also show that the size of product assortment is positively related to the variety of channel mix.

4.3 Existing channel capabilities

Channels differ in the ability to provide information, compare and touch products, and compare prices (Verhoef *et al.*, 2007). For example, customers can more easily obtain information, price comparisons, and assortment-seeking value through the Internet than in traditional channels (Noble *et al.*, 2005), while customers in physical stores can touch, feel, and immediately possess a product. Avery *et al.* (2012) show that adding physical stores to the catalog channel (the Internet) generates cannibalization (synergy) effects because of the higher (lower) overlap of channel capabilities.

4.4   Product categories

Because products differ in complexity, purchase frequency, and tangibility (Konuş *et al.*, 2008), some are better suited to be sold in a specific channel than others (Inman *et al.*, 2004). For example, habitual products with short consumption cycles and high frequency of use (e.g., fresh produce, baby food) fit mobile channels better than products requiring research, planning, and extended consideration because of the limited screen size of a mobile device (Wang *et al.*, 2015). Sensory and intangible products are more suited for online channels because of low search costs and a lower need to experience products (Kollmann *et al.*, 2012; Pauwels *et al.*, 2011), while products with more involvement and experience attributes (e.g., automobiles, perfume) tend to be purchased in physical stores (Chen and Tan, 2004; Gensler *et al.*, 2012b). Chang *et al.* (2016) further reveal that buying products from a "fit" channel can significantly improve customers' trust in retailers and increase their spending.

Kushwaha and Shankar (2013) assess the interaction of different product attributes across channels (i.e., utilitarian vs. hedonic, high- vs. low-risk). They find that low-risk categories have positive effects on value generated by customers who only purchase in traditional channels, while hedonic categories and categories of both low risk and a hedonic nature positively affect value creation of multichannel customers (traditional and Internet-based channels). The authors also show that utilitarian categories with high (low) risk positively affect performance generated by web-only (catalog- or store-only) customers.

4.5   Customer characteristics

Retailers may also change the channel mix as their customers desire the availability of new channels. Individual customers differ in channel preferences because of various characteristics (i.e., geographic characteristics, demographics, and behaviors) (Wilson *et al.*, 2008).

Thus, we discuss drivers of channel additions by considering which customers are more likely to use new (online and mobile) channels.

We consider two geographic characteristics: distance to stores and level of urbanization. Previous research shows that customers who live far away from the closest physical store are more likely to purchase through online and mobile channels (Melis *et al.*, 2016; Venkatesan *et al.*, 2007; Wang and Goldfarb, 2017). Regarding urbanization, Montaguti *et al.* (2015) show that customers in big cities tend to choose more channels when purchasing books, while Konuş *et al.* (2008) do not find a significant effect of urbanization on the number of channels used to buy books, but do so for clothing.

Studies have also explored the effects of age, gender, income, education, and family size as demographic variables. Findings show that young customers tend to use Internet-based channels in general (De Keyser *et al.*, 2015; Narang and Shankar, 2016; Van Nierop *et al.*, 2011; Xue *et al.*, 2011), while customers older than 61 years show the lowest likelihood to purchase via mobile channels because of the high cognitive effort involved in learning how to handle a new technology and their low need for a fast-paced life (Wang *et al.*, 2015). Kushwaha (2007) finds an inverted U-shaped relationship between age and multichannel shopping. Middle-age people are more likely to purchase via multiple channels, while older and younger people have a higher propensity to be offline-only shoppers due to more available time. Other studies show that male customers are more inclined to use new channels than female customers across categories (i.e., health and natural products, video games, electronics and wireless services, and apparel) (Li *et al.*, 2015; Narang and Shankar, 2016; Venkatesan *et al.*, 2007). However, the effect of gender may differ depending on product categories in other cases. Montaguti *et al.* (2015) find that in the book category, women are more likely to use multiple channels to purchase than men. Moreover, customers with higher incomes and higher education show a higher online and multichannel shopping tendency (e.g., Kumar and Venkatesan, 2005; Van Nierop *et al.*, 2011). Kushwaha and Shankar (2013) indicate that customers with a large family size prefer shopping online, while customers without children are more likely to stay offline and less likely to migrate to online channels (Ansari *et al.*, 2008). Nevertheless, some studies do not find significant roles of these demographics in channel choices, as demographics are not strongly related to customer behavior in all contexts (e.g., Kollmann *et al.*, 2012; Konuş *et al.*, 2008).

Retailers should consider several key consumer behaviors as well. Customers with more online experience, higher purchase frequency, higher cross-buying, and a longer relationship are prone to adopt new channels more quickly (Ansari *et al.*, 2008; Frambach *et al.*, 2007; Kumar and Venkatesan, 2005; Narang and Shankar, 2016; Pauwels *et al.*, 2011; Venkatesan *et al.*, 2007). Customers' past returns of products have a U-shaped relationship to the second channel addition but a negative effect on the third channel addition (Venkatesan *et al.*, 2007). We summarize key topics and current findings of each section in Table 4.1.

4.6 Future research

Previous studies provide valuable knowledge of multichannel retailing; still, research gaps can be identified. Meanwhile, multichannel retailing has created many challenges for retailers. Although retailers develop their multichannel marketing strategies cautiously, they still face issues that need to be resolved. In addition, environmental changes due to technological advances (e.g., apps, augmented reality, virtual reality) drive different developments of multichannel retailing. Thus, we systematically derive three research areas that deserve future study: (1) research gaps, (2) unresolved issues in practice, and (3) environment changes (e.g., technological advances). We abbreviate our perspectives as the GUE approach and summarize future research questions for each section in Table 4.2.

4.6.1 Research gaps

The majority of studies have discussed a retailer's decision for channel additions. However, with multichannel retailing becoming the new norm, the question arises if providing customers with multiple channels (e.g., by adding new channels to the mix) will continue to be a value driver for companies, or will multichannel provision become a basic requirement rather than a differentiating factor?

Table 4.1: Summary of key issues and current findings in multichannel retailing

Key topics	Critical questions	Current findings
RQ1. Determinants of retailers' channel choices	• What drives retailers to change their channel mix and add or eliminate channels?	• Little is known about the drivers of retailers' channel choice. Only generic firm strategies and customer orientation are examined in channel additions. • Multiple factors moderate the success of channel additions, including the characteristics of markets, retailers, channels, products, and customers.
RQ2. Determinants of customers' single-channel selections	• What motivates a customer to choose a specific channel to purchase?	• This is almost a mature area for most channels. Customers' channel choices are determined by channel attributes, marketing effort, channel integration, social influence, situational factors, and customer heterogeneity.
RQ3. Multichannel shopping and customer segments	• How do multichannel shoppers behave in their purchase journey? • What are the characteristics do multichannel shoppers? • How do retailers segment customers in multichannel retailing?	• Increasingly more customers are becoming multichannel shoppers. They combine different channels in their single and/or repeated purchases. • Multichannel shoppers' preferences for channels are time- and context-varying. • Customer segments can be identified on the basis of channel categories and the number of channels used in repeated purchases or customers' psychographic and demographic characteristics. • Research-shoppers are an important segment.

Table 4.1: Continued

Key topics	Critical questions	Current findings
RQ4. Multichannel marketing strategies	• How do retailers implement the marketing mix in multichannel retailing? • How do retailers integrate channels in multichannel retailing?	• Multichannel retailers are using many innovative ways to implement strategies of pricing, promotion, assortment, service, and communication across channels. • Marketing effort in one channel affects other channels of the same retailer. • Some studies on channel integration have shown positive effects on retailers' sales growth.
RQ5. Synthesized outcomes of multichannel retailing at the customer level	• What are the effects of multichannel retailing on customer satisfaction and loyalty?	• Multichannel offerings enhance customer satisfaction. • Studies show opposite findings of the effects of a multichannel offering on customer loyalty. • Customers exhibit different levels of satisfaction and loyalty across channels.
RQ6. Synthesized outcomes of multichannel retailing at the retailer and channel levels	• What are the effects of different multichannel activities on retailer performance? • What are the effects of different multichannel activities on the performance of a particular channel?	• Adding or eliminating channels in general creates more profits and revenues for retailers, but this also depends on other factors, such as market competition. • Customers purchasing through Internet-based (vs. offline channels) or multiple channels (vs. single channel) are more valuable. However, multichannel customers is not always the most profitable.

Table 4.2: Summary of future research directions in multichannel retailing

Key topics	Future research directions derived from the GUE approach
RQ1. Determinants of retailers' channel choices	• What drives retailers' channel elimination? (G) • How does channel elimination affect customers' purchase behavior and loyalty to retailers? (G) • Will providing customers with multiple channels continue to serve as a value driver for companies, or will multichannel provision become a basic requirement instead of a differentiating factor? (G) • Whether do potential moderators/drivers play different roles in different channel decisions, i.e., channel addition versus channel elimination? (G) • Why do some retailers maintain a single channel instead of adopting a multichannel strategy, and when will they invest in a multichannel system? (U) • Is there a new taxonomy for channels taking into account different roles of channels in the channel mix? (G) • What drives retailers to assign different weight to the role of channels in their channel mix? (U) • Why do retailers adopt social media as transaction channels, and how should they manage all their channels? (E) • How can retailers make more informed decisions based on the increase of available customer data, for example, using the data of online browsing to improve customers' offline in-store experience? (E)
RQ2. Determinants of customers' single-channel selections	• Substantial articles on this topic can be synthesized in a meta-analysis. (G) • What are the boundary conditions of channel adoption (e.g., time of day, recommended channels)? (G) • Whether and how do drivers play different roles in different channel usage, i.e., purchases versus communications? (G) • Whether and how do drivers differently influences channel adoption across purchase stages? (G) • What drives repeated usage and disadoption of apps? (U) • Is privacy concern a factor inhibiting customer usage of apps? How do consumers response to retailers' marketing activities based on their privacy information, e.g., locations, browsing traces, and social media information? (U) • How do technologies combined in physical stores change customers' attitudes, experiences, and purchase intentions in the store—such as Walmart with kiosks and other retailers' offline stores with the technologies to check price, find items, and redeem discounts? (E)

Table 4.2: Continued

Key topics	Future research directions derived from the GUE approach
	• How do customers perceive physical stores without any employees, such as Tao Cafe launched by the Alibaba Group in China and the coming Amazon Go? (E)
	• Why do customers choose or not choose social media to purchase products when social media has transactional functions? (E)
RQ3. Multichannel shopping and customer segments	• We suggest that studies segment customers from a forward-looking perspective according to preferences, responsiveness, and growth potential. (G)
	• How can the previous segmentation method be put into a measurable, accessible, and actionable scheme that can be applied to a retailer's entire consumer base? (G)
	• How does customers' channel switching behavior during the same purchase journey influence spending and retailer performance? (G)
	• How can retailers provide an approach that can identify and predict customer segments and is also adaptive to dynamic environments? (U)
	• How do retailers estimate financial and nonfinancial benefits generated by each customer segment, how do they provide pertinent marketing efforts in each segment, and how do they manage all segments across channels, products, brands, and so on? (U)
	• Future research should include new channels, such as mobile apps and multiple touchpoints, to identify customer segments and explore customer characteristics and their usage of new channels in each segment. (E)
	• How do research-shoppers evolve, and what are the new patterns of these shoppers with the proliferation of new channels? (E)
	• Which situational factors and customer characteristics can predict different sequences of channel usage in the purchase journey? (E)
	• How do customers use specific functions of Internet-based channels in different contexts, and how does different function usage influence customers' purchase behavior? (E)
RQ4. Multichannel marketing strategies	• How can channel integration be defined and measured? If channel integration can be measured, is there an optimal level of integration? (G)
	• Is there a systematic and standard approach to channel integration that can be applied to all retailers? Or does channel integration depend on contexts instead of being achieved with a standard approach? (G)

Table 4.2: Continued

Key topics	Future research directions derived from the GUE approach
	• How does channel integration affect retailer performance? Does it affect performance directly or indirectly, for example, through customer experience? (G)
	• How does a different marketing mix influence customer experience? (G)
	• How can retailers integrate and optimize customer experiences across channels? (G)
	• How do retailers provide and manage service across channels? (G)
	• What are the roles of service failure, recovery, and guarantees in multichannel retailing? Future studies could test Rust and Huang's (2012) theory. (G)
	• How do retailers evaluate the long-term benefit of channel integration to ensure that such as a strategy will result in long-term profits? (U)
	• How can retailers identify customer needs in each stage of purchase journey and provide targeted strategies? How do retailers evaluate the contribution of marketing strategies in each stage? (U)
	• How can retailers succeed in new marketing activities with advanced technologies (e.g., AR, VR, and 360-degree views), and how do such marketing activities influence customer experiences and retailer performance? (E)
	• How can retailers collect and use big-volume data to profile customers more accurately?
	• How do retailers identify customers' behavioral patterns and use these patterns to provide customers with customized in-store experiences? (E)
	• How can smart technologies be successfully integrated into a retailer's channel mix to improve customers' overall journey experience? (E)
RQ5. Synthesized outcomes of multichannel retailing at the customer level	• What are the general effects of multichannel retailing on customer loyalty? What are the boundaries of different findings in existing studies? (G)
	• How does the adoption of multichannel offerings and channel satisfaction/loyalty interact with each other? What is the role of attitudes in this interaction? (G)
	• Customer experience could be an important antecedent of customer loyalty. How can it be measured and improved in multichannel retailing? (G)
	• Can a multichannel system really increase a focal retailer's customer loyalty, given that all competitors provide multichannel systems? (U)
	• What drives customer loyalty to multichannel retailers in the long run? (U)
	• How do new channels, such as mobile apps, social media, and other touchpoints, influence customer loyalty to retailers, and which retailers specifically benefit? (E)

Table 4.2: Continued

Key topics	Future research directions derived from the GUE approach
RQ6. Synthesized outcomes of multichannel retailing at the retailer and channel levels	• How do advanced technologies (e.g., AR, VR, iPads) in a specific channel affect customers' experiences and their satisfaction/loyalty? (E)
	• What are the effects of multichannel retailing on retailer performance in a long run given that marketing activities have lagged effects and customer behavior changes over time? (G)
	• What is the link between channel loyalty and customer performance in multichannel retailing? (G)
	• What are the cross-channel effects of loyalty on channel performance? (G)
	• How do retailers use a forward-looking metric (e.g., customer lifetime value) to measure and predict customer value across segments? (G)
	• What factors influence multichannel customer profitability? For example, does the context of multichannel adoption influence how profitable a customer becomes? (G)
	• How can retailers improve their competitive advantages by making full use of their experiences in existing channels when adopt a new channel? For example, as an online giant, how does Amazon use its online experiences at physical stores of Whole Foods? For traditional retailers, how do they succeed with lower technological and digital capabilities? (U)
	• Should retailers allow channel cannibalization even if total profit remains stable or increases? (U)
	• Is it always good for retailers to resolve channel cannibalization and synergy? (U)
	• What is the balance between channel cannibalization and synergy? (U)
	• How do retailers allocate their resources with an increasing number of channels and touchpoints, especially by using big data? (U/E)
	• Mobile websites/apps can be a separate purchase channel or an integrated technology in physical stores to facilitate customers' in-store shopping. How and when do websites/mobile apps in such different contexts affect retailer performance? (E)
	• What are the effects of touchpoints and advanced technologies such as IoT, AR, and VR on retailer performance? Is it worth investing in these new digital touchpoints and technologies? (E)

Note: AR = augmented reality, VR = virtual reality, IoT = Internet of Things.

Turning to channel elimination, research is still scant. Only Konuş *et al.*'s (2014) study provides a first investigation into channel elimination. However, their study focuses on how channel elimination influences customers' subsequent purchase behavior and does not discuss the drivers of channel elimination. L Brands, the parent company of Victoria's Secret, recently announced that it will eliminate its famous catalogs because they had little to no impact on product sales (Dostis, 2016). However, L Brands did not consider the role of catalogs as a channel to retain customer; many customers like their famed catalogs even though they did not purchase often through this channel and probably will negatively respond to catalog elimination. Thus, more knowledge of the effects of channel elimination is required. We pose two questions. First, what drives retailers' channel elimination? Potential drivers could be the customer base in a channel, customer preference for and usage of a channel, and the role of a channel in the whole channel system (e.g., sales channel vs. search channel). Second, how does channel elimination influence customers' purchase behavior and loyalty to retailers?

Another interesting and relevant topic is that the moderators or drivers of retailers' channel mix may play different roles for different channel decisions, i.e., channel addition versus channel elimination. For instance, intense competition potentially leads retailers to add new channels as a differentiation mechanism or simply a defensive mechanism to compete with others. However, strong competition might reduce the possibility of eliminating channels because of the fear of losing customers in existing channels to competing retailers, although some existing channels might only create low profit or not generate net margin any more. Such questions should be considered in future research of channel decisions.

4.6.2 Unresolved issues

Some retailers are still operating only a single channel, even though multichannel retailing has become the dominant strategy. These retailers might lose multichannel shoppers and give customers of multichannel competitors extra benefits due to, for example, the showrooming phenomenon (Gensler *et al.*, 2017; Van Baal and Dach, 2005). Do retailers view a single channel as a durable strategy, or will they adopt a multichannel strategy soon? We suggest that future research explore why some retailers maintain a single channel instead of moving to a multichannel strategy. Second, the majority of retailers operating multiple channels might weight these channels differently in terms of their roles in consumers' purchase journey. These different approaches might require a new taxonomy that takes into account different channel roles in the channel mix. Thus, research should determine what drives retailers to assign different weight to the roles of channels in their channel mix.

4.6.3 Environment changes

With the development of new technologies, social media can also provide transactional functions similar to online and mobile channels. For example, customers can directly purchase a product on the Twitter account of Zara after seeing related information on Twitter; they do not necessarily need to switch to another purchase channel to complete the transaction. Given that social media platforms show different attributes (e.g., strong social networks) from websites or retailer apps, the drivers of retailers' choices might also be different. Thus, the question is why retailers adopt social media as transaction channels and how they should manage all channels. Moreover, with the increase of available customer data, more knowledge on how retailers can make more informed decisions based on these data is necessary. Although previous research provides first insights into the impact of different customer patterns on subsequent purchase(-related) behaviors (e.g., Joo *et al.*, 2014), a comprehensive overview of within- and cross-channel effects and how retailers can integrate these findings into their strategic decision making is still lacking.

5

RQ2: Determinants of customers' single-channel selections

The topic of customers' antecedents of channel choices has been popular for a long time. We classify determinants of channel choices into six groups: channel attributes, marketing effort, channel integration, social influence, situational variables, and consumer heterogeneity (Neslin et al., 2006). As we already discussed the role of socio-demographics in the prior section, we do not repeat the respective findings again.

5.1 Channel attributes

Research on channel attributes emphasizes consumer perceptions of channel capabilities and functions. Early research on multichannel retailing addressed the effects of general attributes that can be applied to all channels, such as ease of use, usefulness, enjoyment, risk, and trust, on consumers' channel adoption by employing the technology acceptance model (e.g., Vijayasarathy, 2004), the theory of reasoned action (e.g., Verhoef and Langerak, 2001), the theory of planned behavior (e.g., Shim et al., 2001), and innovation adoption theory (e.g., Chen and Tan, 2004). Later studies continued to apply these theories to focus on new capabilities and functions of online channels, including security and privacy (e.g., Ha and Stoel, 2009), service quality (e.g., Kollmann *et al.*, 2012), information quality (e.g., Noble *et al.*, 2005), the speed of purchase and response time (e.g., Verhoef *et al.*, 2007), convenience (e.g., Kollmann *et al.*, 2012), system accessibility (e.g., Lin and Lu, 2000), website design (e.g., Montoya-Weiss *et al.*, 2003), and price (e.g., Teerling and Huizingh, 2005).

With the appearance of mobile websites and apps, similar studies on general attributes have emerged (e.g., Bruner and Kumar, 2005; Ko *et al.*, 2009; Sultan *et al.*, 2009. For example, usefulness and ease of use mediate the effects of perceived risk and perceived benefits on mobile shopping intentions (Hubert *et al.*, 2017). In addition, the particular characteristics of mobile devices (e.g., smartphones, tablets), including location specificity, portability, and wireless feature, affect customers' intention to use these channels (Shankar and Balasubramanian, 2009). For example, customers' perceived visual complexity of a mobile website due to the relatively smaller mobile screen increases search cost, time, and effort, which subsequently decrease the intention to use the mobile website (Fritz *et al.*, 2017).

5.2   Marketing efforts

Marketing efforts are intended to persuade customers and influence customer behavior in multichannel contexts (Dholakia *et al.*, 2005; Montaguti *et al.*, 2015). Retailers convey information of their products, services, promotions in different channels to potential consumers through marketing activities, such as e-mail and catalogs. Ansari *et al.* (2008) show that marketing communication through e-mail accelerates customer migration to online channels, while marketing communication through catalogs promotes customers' use of catalogs. However, catalogs that remind customers of all a retailer's available channels can improve the likelihood of purchasing in these channels. Kushwaha (2007) finds that catalogs also spur customers to become multichannel shoppers. Moreover, the frequency of sending e-mail and catalogs has a critical and nonlinear effect on consumers' channel adoption (Venkatesan *et al.*, 2007)—it reduces the time of channel adoption when it is below a threshold and increases the adoption duration when it is beyond a certain threshold. The wear-out effect, in which customers respond less to marketing activities over time, also occurs in multichannel contexts (Valentini *et al.*, 2011).

5.3   Channel integration

Integration across channels helps consumers perceive more consistency and less confusion. It caters to customers' needs for a seamless experience during multichannel shopping (Melero *et al.*, 2016). Cao and Li (2015) provide detailed evidence of the positive effect of channel integration, which can be explained by four mechanisms. The authors argue that channel integration positively influences a retailer's overall sales growth by improving consumer trust, improving customer loyalty, increasing conversion rates, and providing more opportunities to cross-sell. At the channel level, Herhausen *et al.* (2015) report that integrating access to and knowledge about an offline store into an online channel increases the perceived quality of the focal website and leads to more online purchases. Melis *et al.* (2015) also show that consumers prefer a newly added website that offers a similar assortment to the offline channels of the same retailer, as consumers are more familiar with such an online shopping environment and perceive lower risk when they purchase in the new channel.

5.4   Social influence

Customers' channel choices are also affected by the interaction in social networks (Verhoef *et al.*, 2007). Studies reveal that interactions between customers who can be observed in the same consumption environment influence their purchase consideration of products and brands (Baxendale *et al.*, 2015; Wang *et al.*, 2012). Bilgicer *et al.* (2015) detail that a customer's network peers, who live in close proximity and are similar to him or her, are easier to communicate with and share purchase experience, thus influencing his or her adoption of a new channel. More importantly, the effects of geographic proximity on such imitation behavior of online channel usage in one's social network decrease over time, while the effects of similarity among individuals on such imitation behavior have a rising trend (Choi *et al.*, 2010).

5.5   Situational factors

Situational factors cover environmental conditions and temporal issues in extant research. Environmental conditions influencing channel choice refer to the environment in which consumers access a specific channel, "together with any complicating factors arising from the intervening technologies" (Nicholson *et al.*, 2002, p. 134), including weather, mobility, distance, crowdedness, and visible configurations of channels. Andrews *et al.* (2015) and Li *et al.* (2017) show that increased physical crowding and sunny weather make consumers more susceptible and respond more to mobile promotions, respectively. Regarding temporal issues, the urgency of purchase is significant. Customers under larger pressure of limited time are more likely to purchase in Internet-based channels due to the convenience of use and the accessibility at any time and place (Konuş *et al.*, 2008; Melis *et al.*, 2016). Studies also suggest that holidays and event proximity, such as date relative to "pay day," can affect customers' channel choices (e.g., Nicholson *et al.*, 2002; Van Nierop *et al.*, 2011; Wang *et al.*, 2015).

5.6   Consumer heterogeneity

In addition to the heterogeneity of customer demographics and past behaviors mentioned in RQ1, customer psychographics lead to distinct intrinsic preferences for a certain channel (Konuş *et al.*, 2008). We discuss multiple variables that have been studied. First, online self-efficacy, defined as "a consumer's self-assessment of his/her capabilities to shop online" (Vijayasarathy, 2004, p. 751), can improve consumers' preference for online shopping (O'Cass and Fenech, 2003). Second, Bruner and Kumar (2005) find that consumers who are more predisposed toward a visual model have a higher tendency to adopt Internet-based channels because they tend to process information by mental imagery and are more attracted by visual cues (e.g., icons, symbols) than low-visual consumers. Third, consumers with higher price sensitivity tend to choose online channels more often because of the convenience of price comparisons and an overall lower perceived price (Degeratu *et al.*, 2000; Lynch and Ariely, 2000). Fourth, goal-oriented consumers are more likely to use online channels, which ease the search for information and thus save time; while experiential-oriented consumers are more prone to use catalogs and physical stores because they can experience enjoyment of shopping in traditional channels (Pauwels and Neslin, 2015).

5.7 Future research

5.7.1 Research gaps

Numerous studies have explored the antecedents of customers' channel choices, making it a rather mature research area. First, a meta-analysis on this topic would be valuable to provide generalized conclusions (Verhoef *et al.*, 2015). Second, the potential boundary conditions of channel adoption have not been discussed. For example, the time of day could have an influence on channel choices. Consumers likely turn to online channels outside regular opening hours of physical stores. People on the way to work likely browse news on their smartphones in the morning; thus, they might also be more likely to shop on their smartphones as only their smartphones are available at that point. People working in an office during the day might shop on their work computers, while they might play games or chat with others on their smartphones before going to bed at night and thus are more likely to use their smartphones to shop at that time. Another potential boundary condition is the channel through which a purchase link is recommended by retailers, brands, or friends. For example, a consumer who receives a product link through WhatsApp or WeChat will probably open the purchase link and not switch to other channels to avoid extra switching costs because he or she trusts the provided information source. Similarly, if retailers or brands recommend a purchase link to consumers through e-mail, consumers might use websites to purchase when they read their e-mail on their PCs.

Antecedents of channel choices might influence customers differently according to channel usage, i.e., purchases versus communications. Polo and Sese (2016) explore and reveal different roles of same drivers played in channel decisions of purchasing and communicating. They show that prior experience, customer attitude, and offline-channel preference play more important roles in purchasing channel decisions, while marketing activities and online-channel preference drive more communication-related channel choices. The authors contribute to our understanding of customers' channel choices in different situations, but more related research is needed in the future.

Customers also behave differently across purchase stages in shopping journey (e.g., Lemon and Verhoef, 2016). For example, consumers may choose channels based on their prior experience in the pre-purchase stage, or being influenced by retailers' marketing effort like advertisements. In the purchase stage, consumers' channel choices might depend more on the association between product categories and channel attributes, peer contagion, and also marketing activities like coupons. Post-purchase stage involves both purchase-related activities (e.g., consumption, product return, service request) and non-purchase behaviors (e.g., word of mouth). Purchase-related behaviors shape customer experience and lay the foundation of customers' further engagement. Moreover, consumers might be triggered to become loyal or start new purchase processes in this stage. However, little research differentiates purchase stages when studying drivers of customers' channel choices. We thereby urge future research to contribute to this topic and refine antecedent differences in purchase journey.

5.7.2   Unresolved issues

Mobile apps are important for mobile channels. However, approximately 20% of apps are only used once after being downloaded (Hoch, 2014), and 50% of customers will delete an app if they find it does not work properly (SmartBear, 2014). It seems that stickiness of apps is a problem for retailers. Further research on the drivers of repeated usage and disadoption of apps is required (Prins *et al.*, 2009).

Another related question is apps' dark side, namely, privacy issues. More and more retailers are adopting apps to attract and engage customers. One of the advantages of marketing in apps is to develop personalized strategies for individuals based on customers' personal information (e.g., email address, phone number, location), searching and purchasing histories, external information derived from one's social media, etc. However, such information and data is highly connected to customer privacy and may trigger customers' perception of intrusiveness (e.g., Van Doorn and Hoekstra, 2013; for a literature review, see Beke *et al.*, 2018). Thus privacy information collected and used by retailers might be a concern inhibiting customer usage of apps. Furthermore, it also influences customers' reactions to retailers' marketing efforts and probably reduce the effectiveness of personalized strategies when privacy related information is very sensitive or not used in an appropriate approach. We suggest future studies on mobile apps pay more attention on privacy issues and related consequences on customer responses to retailers' marketing activities.

5.7.3   Environment changes

Retailers are integrating more technologies in their offline stores to improve customer experience. For example, since 2017 Walmart has installed in-store pick-up kiosks (Retail Customer Experience, 2017). Customers can scan a barcode located on their purchase receipts and receive items appearing on a conveyor belt within 45 seconds. These new technologies pose the following research question: How do such technologies combined in physical stores change customers' attitudes, experiences, and purchase intentions offline? An extreme example is when technology in-store replaces all employees, such as in the case of the Alibaba Group in China, which publicly opened the physical store Tao Cafe without any employees on July 8, 2017 (Liangyu, 2017). A similar store concept is the upcoming Amazon Go (Retail Customer Experience, 2016). However, this is a new retailing phenomenon that has not been discussed in research. More knowledge of marketing in physical stores without any employees is required. For example, how will customers perceive and adopt them? In addition to advanced physical stores, knowledge is required on why customers choose or do not choose to purchase products on social media if social media has transactional functions.

6

RQ3: Multichannel shopping and customer segments

6.1 Multichannel shopping

Only one of three shoppers exhibited a single-channel shopping style, with the other two-thirds regularly using more channels to shop, according to an online study by the Baker Retailing Center (2012); another recent study showed that 73% of customers used multiple channels during their purchase journey (Sopadjieva *et al.*, 2017). The phenomenon of multichannel shopping is well-established, as it can satisfy consumers' different needs and preferences in various contexts and along the purchase journey (Verhoef *et al.*, 2007). For example, a customer might try on a dress and buy it immediately in one of Zara's offline stores, search and buy a book on Amazon's website, or buy a movie ticket with her smartphone; this customer can also buy the dress on Zara's website when she is in the office or through Zara's app when she is on the subway.

Multichannel shoppers may have no certain preference for a particular channel consistently, but rather their preferences are time- and context-varying. Their demands are indeed dynamic and changing, which is contingent on all the internal and external circumstances discussed previously in RQ2. Konuş *et al.* (2008) find that consumers prefer using multiple channels to buy low-touch products (without the need for inspection before purchase; e.g., airline tickets, software) to high-touch products (e.g., clothing, health products) because they value the convenience and quick purchasing. Multichannel behavior can be significantly boosted by marketing campaigns stressing multichannel benefits without financial incentives (Montaguti *et al.*, 2015). In general, consumers can purchase through a combined channel mix to fulfill multiple internal needs, such as emotional and social needs in physical stores and convenience and independence in Internet-based channels (Schröder and Zaharia, 2008).

6.2 Customer segments

Retailers need to reach the right customers with their channel approach and identify characteristics and needs of specific customer segments, which is a key goal of retailers' multichannel strategies (Konuş *et al.*, 2008; Wilson *et al.*, 2008). The primary differentiation of customer segments is based on channel categories and the number of channels adopted in customers' repeat purchases (see Table 6.1) (McGoldrick and Collins, 2007; Montaguti *et al.*, 2015). For example, multichannel shoppers express positive attitudes toward all channels and are much younger than other segments (McGoldrick and Collins, 2007).

Konuş *et al.* (2008) identify three customer segments for offline stores, catalogs, and the Internet across several categories. The first segment is uninvolved shoppers, who neither rate any channel highly for two stages of the purchase journey (i.e., search and purchase) nor show an unequivocal preference for multichannel shopping. They exhibit low loyalty, low shopping enjoyment, relatively lower price consciousness, and slightly higher innovativeness. The second segment is multichannel enthusiasts. They have strong positive attitudes toward the three channels for search and transaction and show low loyalty but high innovativeness and high shopping enjoyment. The third segment consists of store-focused shoppers, who exhibit high loyalty, relatively high shopping enjoyment, and low innovativeness. This segment has a clear preference for physical stores but hold unfavorable attitudes toward other channels.

Table 6.1: Multichannel selection and customer segments

Articles	Purchase stage			Segments			
Multichannel selection for different purchases							
Schoenbachler and Gordon, 2002	×						
Kumar and Venkatesan, 2005	×						
Venkatesan et al., 2007	×						
McGoldrick and Collins, 2007 (survey)	N = **2,340**			Stores-prone shoppers 61.9%	Catalog-prone shoppers 6.4%	Internet-prone shoppers 9.3%	Multichannel shoppers 22.4%
Montaguti et al., 2015	N = **30,710** ×			No-purchase customer 31.4%	Single-channel shoppers 61.3%	Two-channel shoppers 6.7%	Three-channel shoppers 0.6%
Multichannel selection in different purchase stages of the same purchase journey **(1: information search; 2: purchase; 3: aftersales)**	1	2	3				
Verhoef et al., 2007	×	×					
Dholakia et al., 2005	×	×	×				
Voorveld et al., 2016	×	×	×				
Van Baal and Dach (2005)	N = **1,094**			Shoppers without channel switch 69.2%	Research shoppers at a retailer 10.4%	Research shoppers at two retailers 20.4%	
Schröder and Zaharia (2008)	×	N = **525**		Single-channel users 67.4%	Research shoppers 32.6%		
Konuş et al. (2008)	×	N = **360**		Uninvolved shoppers 40%	Multichannel enthusiasts 37%	Store-focused shoppers 23%	
Gensler et al. (2017)	×	N = **556**	×	Competitive showroomers 26.3%	Nonshowroomers 73.7%		

Table 6.1: Continued

Articles	Purchase stage		Segments				
	N = 314	Research shoppers		Web-focused shoppers		Store-focused shoppers	Call center-prone shoppers
		After sales: store	After sales: Internet/store	After sales: web	After sales: store/call center		
De Haan *et al.* (2015)	× × ×	35%	11%	22%	9%	18%	6%

Note: N is the sample size.

De Keyser *et al.* (2015) extend Konuş *et al.*'s (2008) study by including an after-sales stage, a call center channel, and more covariates (e.g., product complexity) to predict customer segments. They refine the multichannel enthusiasts as research-shoppers and web-focused shoppers and further differentiate the two segments into subgroups according to the channel used in the after-sales stage. The authors also identify an important segment of call center–prone shoppers. Compared with covariates in Konuş *et al.*'s (2008) study, customer loyalty and perceived complexity of products predict customer segments in De Keyser *et al.*'s (2015) work, but innovativeness is not significant.

Research-shoppers are a special segment because they switch channels during the purchase journey. Research-shoppers search information in one channel but accomplish final transactions in another channel (Verhoef *et al.*, 2007). This segment occupies more than 30% of the total customer sample in related studies (e.g., Schröder and Zaharia, 2008) (see Table 6.1), with some customers in this segment being free riders (Van Baal and Dach, 2005). Free riders search in one channel of retailer A but purchase in another channel of retailer B. Verhoef *et al.* (2007) offer three mechanisms that explain the research-shopping phenomenon. The first is channel-stage association, or the perceived matching association between channel attributes and customer needs in a specific purchase stage. The second mechanism is channel lock-in. A high lock-in channel has enough stickiness to keep customers who both search and purchase products in it instead of switching to another channel after searching information. Thus, research-shopping is more likely to occur in low lock-in channels. For example, the Internet has a low lock-in level because of the ease of exiting and the perception of information source in customers' minds. The third mechanism is cross-channel synergy, indicating that searching in one channel improves the experience of purchasing in another channel.

Research-shopping can be further grouped into two opposite behaviors: web rooming and showrooming. With web rooming, consumers search information on websites and purchase products or services in offline stores (Phillips, 2013), which enables them to combine the independence and convenience of searching information online with the decreased risks of buying offline (Schröder and Zaharia, 2008).

Conversely, showroomers view products in a physical store and later buy through the online channel (Butler, 2013; Wolny and Charoensuksai, 2016). Recently, research has associated competitive showrooming with free-riding behavior and defined it as searching in an offline channel of retailer A but purchasing online at retailer B (Chiu *et al.*, 2011; Gensler *et al.*, 2017). Daunt and Harris (2017) argue that in a situation of competitive showrooming, consumers use offline resources provided by retailer A but do not purchase from it, which damages A's benefits but is conducive to retailer B. Daunt and Harris demonstrate that characteristics of consumers, channels, and products are critical antecedents of the value damage and creation of showrooming for different channels and retailers. Gensler *et al.* (2017) further show that a higher perceived price dispersion in an online channel leads to price comparisons and accelerates competitive showrooming. Gensler *et al.* find that lower perceived average prices, higher quality in the online channel, and long waiting times to receive help in a physical store are positively related to showrooming.

Consumers may also use different channels in the after-sales stage of the purchase funnel. Even consumers who search and purchase on websites do not necessarily go to websites to obtain after-sales services. Rather, approximately 30% of these customers choose stores or call centers in the after-sales stage (De Keyser *et al.*, 2015), probably because they need human contact to deal with complex issues related to consumption. However, more Internet experience could improve the usage intention for online channels in the after-sales stage (Frambach *et al.*, 2007).

6.3   Future research

6.3.1   Research gaps

Previous research has segmented consumers according to channel usage and psychographics. This segmentation only considers customers' current characteristics; however, according to Neslin and Shankar (2009), another promising approach to segment customers is to take into account a more forward-looking perspective. Neslin and Shankar suggest that customers differ not only in their intrinsic channel preferences and responses to marketing efforts but also in their growth potential (i.e., based on purchase quantity, timing, returns, and margin), which includes rich information for predicting future behavior. Thus, integrating perspectives of preferences, responsiveness, and growth potential to segment customers would provide more insights and should be explored in future studies. Accordingly, this begs the question of how this segmentation method can be put into a measurable, accessible, and actionable scheme that can be applied to a retailer's entire customer base.

In all the customer segments identified in previous studies, research-shoppers are notable (Verhoef *et al.*, 2007). However, previous studies on research-shoppers only use survey data and do not link this phenomenon with customers' real purchase behavior. Thus, future research could explore how customers' channel-switching behavior during the same purchase journey influences their spending and retailer performance.

6.3.2 Unresolved issues

Given rapidly evolving markets and customers, multichannel retailers are faced with the challenge of accurately identifying customer segments. To be responsive to this dynamic environment, however, retailers need an approach with stronger predictive ability for customer segments (Neslin and Shankar, 2009). After identifying different customer segments, retailers still face the challenges of how to estimate financial and nonfinancial benefits generated by each segment, how much marketing efforts should be expended in each segment, how to manage all segments across channels, product categories, brands, and so on.

6.3.3 Environment changes

The most significant change of technology advances is related to mobile apps, social media, and other digital touchpoints. First, regarding customer segments, the proliferation of these new channels leads to changes in purchase-related behavior. Future research should take into account new channels to identify customer segments and explore customer characteristics and new channel usage in each segment. The increasing use of multiple touchpoints in an omnichannel environment also calls for new segmentation studies (Verhoef *et al.*, 2015). Studies should also consider competitive touchpoints and channel usage.

Second, we might also expect research-shoppers' behavioral patterns to evolve with the proliferation of new channels. For example, a consumer might search information online and later make a purchase through a smartphone while being on the go or on a computer. This situation differs from web roomers and showroomers discussed in previous studies. Therefore, we encourage future research to identify more patterns of research-shoppers. Moreover, what situational factors and customer characteristics can predict different sequences of channel usage during consumers' purchase journey? How do consumers' experiences in one channel influence their perceptions of subsequent channel touchpoints?

Third, in focusing on one channel—mobile apps—most research has so far concentrated on whether a purchase took place through an app (e.g., Wang *et al.*, 2015), but little is known about which app features (e.g., information look-up, check-in, loyalty program, promotion offer, customer services) consumers use in different contexts and how their usage influences subsequent purchase-related behaviors. Kim *et al.* (2015) find that using the feature of information look-up or location check-in can increase customers' future spending and using the combination of the two features can increase spending more than only using one feature. However, they broadly define information look-up, which makes it unclear whether a customer is searching a product, checking point balances, or browsing reward items, etc., when he or she is looking up information on the app. Future research should explore how customers use specific functions of Internet-based channels in different contexts and how different function usage influences customers' purchase behavior.

7

RQ4: Multichannel marketing strategies

The strategies of multichannel marketing can be categorized into the marketing mix and channel integration (Friedman and Furey, 2003). For the marketing mix, channels of the same retailer are independent of one another and separately provide a package of services that target certain customer segments. For channel integration, channels are not independent and offer joint services with links to other channels.

7.1 Marketing mix

Decisions regarding the multichannel marketing mix focus on pricing, promotion, assortment, communication, and service across channels in specific stages of the purchase funnel (Verhoef, 2012). We expand on these components of the marketing mix next.

7.1.1 Pricing

Most multichannel retailers set the same price across channels to avoid any perceived inconsistency and dissatisfaction, while other retailers apply channel-based price discrimination (Wolk and Ebling, 2010). Empirical studies show that Internet-based channels set lower prices than physical stores on average, probably because of higher perceived risk and lower searching cost on the Internet (e.g., Ratchford, 2009; Wolk and Ebling, 2010). Li and Tang (2011) compare multichannel and online-only retailers and find that the former differentiate themselves from pure online retailers on nonprice dimensions and thus set higher prices.

Price discounts are a popular pricing strategy in multichannel retailing. However, Breugelmans and Campo (2016) find that price promotions in one channel can have negative effects on purchases in the other channel because customers reallocate their spending depending on promotions to maximize their benefit. Channel attributes (e.g., convenience and no travel costs in online channels) could lead to asymmetric effects; for example, Breugelmans and Campo show that online price promotions have a stronger negative impact on offline purchase than offline promotions have on online purchase. Some retailers choose to advertise in-store prices online to shift purchases to offline because an online channel can well exhibit price information of all products and effectively target online customers. Zhang (2009) maintains that this strategy is useful only when the online margin is low because, in this case, the shifting to offline can generate higher profits. Prior research has recently proposed some pricing innovations like dynamic pricing models based on technology advances and rich data in multichannel contexts (for a review, see Grewal *et al.*, 2011).

7.1.2 Promotion

Research shows that different promotions across channels interact with one another. For example, promotions in physical stores affect not only store purchases but also purchases in catalogs and on the Internet (Pauwels and Neslin, 2015). Olbrich and Schultz (2014) find that print advertising can stimulate the click-through rate and conversion of search engine advertising, as search engines navigate print media consumers to the advertised website. Naik and Peters (2009) conduct a generalized study on the interaction of offline (television, print, and radio) and online (banners and search) advertisements and find significant synergy effects among all the advertisements. They also reveal that offline/online advertisements can drive customer visits in both offline and online channels. Furthermore, Lobschat *et al.* (2017) suggest that for non-recent online customers, both banner and television advertisements can activate awareness of the advertised products, thus driving website visits and indirectly improving offline sales through website visits. However, banner ads are not effective for recent online consumers, while television ads can still remind these customers of the advertising retailer. Therefore, banner ads do not affect recent online customers' website visits, but television ads increase the likelihood of an offline purchase for these customers.

Retailers also use customized promotions to take advantage of the increasing amount of individual data available in the multichannel environment. Customized promotions (promotions provided to selected consumers) can be implemented at three levels of granularity: a mass-market level, a segment level, and an individual level. In general, performance improvements for customized promotions with more granular levels are small but reply on product categories and shopping venue (Zhang and Wedel, 2009). Zhang and Wedel (2009) also show that loyalty promotions targeting customers who purchased a specific product before the promotion, are more valuable for online stores; while competitive promotions, which target customers who did not purchase a specific product before the promotion, are more effective for offline stores.

Multichannel retailers are also widely delivering mobile promotions through short message services, in-app messaging, social media, e-mail, or push or pull notifications. Mobile promotions aim to incentive a specific consumer response in the short run (for a review, see Andrews *et al.*, 2016). Consumer responses here might be to visit a physical store, make an in-store purchase, share product/service or location-based information through social media, or try new products. For example, mobile coupons can be sent when customers swipe their smartphones at mall entrances by using location-based technologies to attract them to purchase offline. Danaher *et al.* (2015) show that offline redemptions of mobile coupons in this case vary by location and time of delivery, expiry lengths, face values, and product categories.

7.1.3   Assortment

Different assortments across channels may lead to consumer confusion, cognitive overload, distrust, and frustration (Neslin and Shankar, 2009), especially when customers initially shop in multiple channels (Melis *et al.*, 2015). However, each channel has different attributes, costs, competitions, and target customers. Distinct assortments in different channels can also complement one another and extend retailers' product coverage; thus, it is reasonable to differentiate assortments across channels (Berry *et al.*, 2010; Neslin and Shankar, 2009). One popular differentiation strategy is asymmetric assortment. Retailers carry larger product assortments online than offline because of lower search costs for customers in online channels. Offering a large assortment online also allows for lower inventory and less space constraints than in the offline setting (Zhang *et al.*, 2010). For example, Ma (2016) argues that retailers can benefit from offering both main and niche products in their online channel but only main products in the catalog channel. Emrich *et al.* (2015) explore the effects of asymmetric assortment by comparing it with both an identical assortment and an entirely different assortment across channels for different retailers. The authors that asymmetrical assortments have advantages only for general retailers providing independent products (e.g., a DVD player and a vase) but have detrimental effects on limited-line retailers providing substitutive products (e.g., different DVD players).

Another assortment decision concerns the design of assortments across channels. Retailers can use a prototypical design to offer a channel-specific format for online shops with standardized and conventional presentations of assortments. They can also use a homogeneous design to offer similar assortments across channels, typically using the offline design as the leader (Emrich and Verhoef, 2015). In their study, Emrich and Verhoef (2015) show that store-oriented customers prefer homogeneous designs, but this preference is offset by competitive price cues online.

7.1.4   Communication

In addition to the function of search and purchase, retailers provide two-way communication in Internet-based channels to reach and interact with customers (Verhoef *et al.*, 2015). Retailers can provide both machine and person interactivity in online and mobile channels (Gu *et al.*, 2013). Machine interactivity refers to interactions between humans and the medium, such as the provision of keyword search on websites and store locators in mobile devices, whereas person interactivity refers to interactions between people through the medium such as click to call and live chat. Gu *et al.* (2013) find that web machine interactivity and mobile person interactivity positively influence retailer sales. However, web machine interactivity has a stronger impact than mobile machine interactivity because web interfaces with large screens better match consumers' search information and processing tasks (Ghose and Park, 2013). Conversely, mobile devices have greater flexibility in dynamic and complex contexts (De Haan *et al.*, 2015) and are easier for consumers to interact with service representatives by clicking to call.

7.1.5 Service

The literature on service across channels is relatively scant. Sousa and Voss (2006) propose three types of service in a multichannel environment: virtual services (based on the Internet), physical services (people-delivered, including logistics), and integration services (seamless service experience across channels). Keeping the same service level across channels is extremely difficult for retailers. First, service in each channel differs in terms of ambient factors, design factors, and social factors (Baker, 1986). For example, retailers offer face-to-face contact and immediate response of employees to customers in offline stores but in most cases, self-service without actual employee interaction in Internet-based channels. Retailers' services also differ in product characteristics—they provide interpersonal contacts for nonroutine or complex products and convenient self-service for routine or normal products (Van Birgelen *et al.*, 2006). Second, retailers may try to provide different or limited service levels across channels to point customers into a certain direction (Montoya-Weiss *et al.*, 2003). Third, consumers have different perceptions of and sensitivity to service levels across channels. For example, some consumers value physical experiences more than others (Dumrongsiri *et al.*, 2008; Montoya-Weiss *et al.*, 2003).

Lund and Marinova (2014) also document that service performance has different effects on retailer revenues across channels. They detail that in physical stores, objective service performance, or "the observable unbiased outcome of the firm's service operation processes and initiatives" (p. 103), positively affects retailer revenues; while in remote channels (i.e., Internet-based channels, television), there is no significant effect. However, the interaction between perceived service and direct marketing affects revenues in both physical and remote channels. Perceptions of service design quality enhance the impact of direct marketing on revenues of physical channels, while lower perceptions of time and effort costs do so in remote channels.

7.2 Channel integration

Channel integration is a challenging issue for retailers because each channel is likely to be governed by different managers, who aim to optimize profits for a specific channel (Verhoef, 2012). Bendoly *et al.* (2005, p. 314) define channel integration as "the use of multiple modes of fulfillment for mutual support of, or as semi-interchangeable alternatives for, end-customers transactions." Retailers can integrate access to and knowledge about an offline channel into an online channel, for example, by providing online search functions, such as availability check and researching products, in their physical stores (Herhausen *et al.*, 2015). Retailers can also allow customers to order products online and pick them up in offline shops or buy products online but return offline (Gallino *et al.*, 2016). Gao and Su (2017) find that the service of buying online and picking up in stores helps expand retailers' market coverage by attracting customers via offering real-time inventory information and avoiding shipping cost. However, this service is not suitable for bestsellers in stores because it weakens the ability to attract consumers to stores. Other research reveals that channel integration, such as sharing information, integrating prices and category assortments, and offering functions not available in other channels (e.g., ship-to-store), increases retailers' sales growth and sales dispersion (Cao and Li, 2015; Gallino *et al.*, 2016; Melis *et al.*, 2016).

7.3 Future research

7.3.1 Research gaps

Multichannel marketing strategy is a topic worthy of future research, and we derive two directions from existing research. The first pertains to channel integration and customer experience. Several studies find that channel integration increases retailer sales. However, multiple questions still remain unanswered. For example, how can channel integration be defined and measured? If the extent of channel integration can be measured, is there an optimal level of integration? Is there a systematic and standard approach to channel integration which can be applied to all retailers, or does channel integration depend on contexts instead of a standard approach? How do customers perceive different approaches to channel integration? How does channel integration influence retailer performance? Does it affect retailer performance directly or indirectly, for example, through customer experience? An appropriate integration could provide a seamless experience for customers (Melero *et al.*, 2016) and thus increase their spending. Little is known about how a multichannel marketing mix influences customer experience. Thus, research could examine how retailers can integrate customer experience across channels for optimization in multichannel retailing.

Second, within the multichannel marketing mix, research on the role of services in multichannel retailing is relatively scant. However, the idea of better serving customers in marketing has become increasingly strong (Grewal and Levy, 2007; Lusch and Vargo, 2011). Furthermore, rich and advanced technologies and the corresponding automation put service in a more salient position in retailing. On one side, automation creates many opportunities for customers to serve themselves during purchase journey. On the other side, poor customer service and service failure (e.g., waiting a long time in automated telephone systems, website crashes) lead to customer frustration and possible switching to other providers. To solve this dilemma, Rust and Huang (2012) propose a theory of optimal service productivity, which differentiates between short-term effects (a trade-off between the use of personnel and automation) and long-term effects (based on how advanced the technology is). Rust and

Huang's research also determines the conditions under which an optimal level of service productivity should be higher or lower. We call for more studies to test Rust and Huang's theory by exploring how to provide and manage service experience across channels and expounding on service failures, recovery, and guarantees in multichannel retailing.

7.3.2   Unresolved issues

The cost of channel integration is a big issue for retailers in the short run, while the accumulated benefit from satisfying customer needs for a seamless experience can be achieved in the long run. How can retailers evaluate the short-term cost and benefit of integration to ensure that this strategy will result in long-term profits?

Lemon and Verhoef (2016) suggest that retailers should identify key elements in each stage of customer journey by incorporating firm and customer perspectives. To develop effective and efficient multichannel strategies, retailers should track customers' shopping process and identify specific purchase stages to understand and satisfy customer needs at a given point and also predict their future needs. However, it seems to need advanced technologies and strong analytical tools to achieve this, which is a big challenge both for retailers to implement and for researchers to evaluate contributions of multichannel strategies in each purchase stage.

7.3.3   Environment changes

Technological progress has enabled retailers to implement new marketing activities and channel integration formats. On the one hand, although many commentators had envisioned "the death of physical stores" after the appearance of Internet-based channels, physical stores have not faded away and are garnering attention again. A case in point is the online giant Amazon, who has stepped into opening offline book stores since 2015. Moreover, according to the study by Bouncepad, most customers want extended digital experience in stores and are more likely to purchase in physical stores offering self-serve or assisted tablets (Earley, 2017). In essence, retailers are integrating new technologies into their offline stores to improve customer experiences. For example, the retailer

Athleta places iPads and digital kiosks near offline checkout desks to prompt customers to search online to select free shipping to their homes (Schiff, 2015). Retailers can also attach QR codes to particular online information or coupons in offline stores. Location-based technologies such as iBeacon help retailers track customer information through smartphones and send personalized discounts based on customers' target products and their location in a store. Retailers such as Cabela's display user-generated content (e.g., online reviews in physical stores) or allow mobile payments to save consumers time in long lines. Moreover, they can use technologies of virtual or augmented reality in offline stores to improve shopping enjoyment. For example, Samsung provides a virtual reality experience at AT&T stores, where customers can try on a Samsung Gear VR to take a virtual Carnival Cruise. A recent study also predicts that the majority of retailers will be able to customize customers' offline store visits through the use of customer data by 2021, an approach called micro-locationing (Columbus, 2017).

On the other hand, retailers are improving consumers' online purchasing experiences by using advanced technologies and combining services from offline channels. For example, Amazon has offered drone delivery since 2016 to provide products faster. On websites, retailers post frequently asked questions on product pages and offer more contact points, such as Live Chat and e-mail, to answer customers' questions as soon as possible, given online customers cannot feel real products and thus have more questions about them. Some retailers create a 360-degree view of store or product images to enhance vividness of customer online experiences. A study by Mindtree (2015) shows that a 360-degree view with good zoom quality is one of the highest-ranked features influencing online purchase and improves customers' connection with retailers.

Although many of these activities are in the experimental stage, they forebode marketing trends and future customer behavior to a great extent. Future research should explore how retailers can successfully implement these activities and also assess how these activities influence customer experience and retailer performance. For example, one question is how retailers can collect and use big-volume data (both structured and unstructured) to profile customers more accurately. In addition, research that provides insights into customers' behavioral patterns and how retailers can use these patterns to provide a promising and customized in-store experience is required. Moreover, how can retailers successfully integrate smart technologies, such as autonomously driving cars or smart refrigerators, into the channel mix to improve customers' overall journey experience?

8

RQ5: Synthesized outcomes of multichannel retailing at the customer level

8.1 Customer level

Both retailers and researchers want to know whether investments in multiple channels can substantially improve customer satisfaction and loyalty. Studies show a positive (or at least a potential) effect of a multichannel offering on overall customer satisfaction and loyalty (e.g., Falk *et al.*, 2007; Ghaleno *et al.*, 2016; Hitt and Frei, 2002; Shankar *et al.*, 2003; Venkatesan *et al.*, 2007). The rationale is that multichannel retailers provide more access to their brands, products, and services than single-channel retailers, thus creating diverse and more flexible choices of buying, paying, and delivering for customers. These elements help retailers better satisfy customer demands. From customers' perspective, they can use different channels in different contexts (e.g. time, locations, purposes), given the distinct advantages of each channel, and experience cross-channel synergies. Taken together, a multichannel setting can serve to enhance customer satisfaction and loyalty (Wallace *et al.*, 2004). Furthermore, the positive relationship between a multichannel offering and customer satisfaction and loyalty can be intensified by improving service quality in all channels (Lin, 2012; Montoya-Weiss *et al.*, 2003), providing interactive advertising (Shen *et al.*, 2016), and integrating channels in an appropriate way (Bendoly *et al.*, 2005; Herhausen *et al.*, 2015).

However, opposite findings also exist. Van Baal and Dach (2005) argue that the multichannel setting of a retailer could erode customer loyalty because the availability of Internet-based channels increases price transparency and decreases switching cost, which increase customers' probability of switching to competitors. Ansari *et al.* (2008) also report decreasing loyalty of customers who migrated to the online channel.

Furthermore, research indicates that customers exhibit different levels of satisfaction across channels. Falk *et al.* (2007) find that offline satisfaction cannibalizes online satisfaction because the former increases perceived risks and decreases perceived usefulness in an online channel. In terms of mobile channels, customers perceive higher valuations of products and marketing activities, leading to greater satisfaction in touch-based mobile devices than in mouse-based computers due to enhanced perceptions of psychological ownership in mobile devices (Brasel and Gips, 2014, 2015).

Other studies demonstrate that customers show loyalty discrimination across channels due to different channel attributes. Verhoef and Donkers (2005) find a negative (positive) relationship between catalogs (websites) used as an acquisition channel and customer loyalty in several industries. They provide evidence that catalogs that focus heavily on lower price attract less loyal customers, while websites provide retailers with economic and social bonds and foster customer loyalty. Moreover, Shankar *et al.* (2003) find that customer loyalty increases when service is established through an online rather than an offline channel in a travel industry. Melis *et al.* (2016) confirm this finding in a grocery retailing context. Melis *et al.* indicate that after the first several purchases online, online purchasing quickly becomes a habitual behavior and customers tend to remain loyal. However other studies show that customers using physical stores and call centers have greater loyalty than customers staying online because the latter are more likely to switch channels or retailers (De Keyser *et al.*, 2015; Konuş *et al.*, 2008).

8.2 Future research

8.2.1 Research gaps

Studies show opposite findings of the effects of multichannel offerings on customer loyalty. Future research should clarify the relationship between multichannel settings and customer loyalty and reveal the boundary conditions of the different findings in previous studies. In addition, customers who are more satisfied with and loyal to a retailer are more likely to accept new channels because they have confidence in the retailer and may perceive less risk when using the new channels. For example, Melis *et al.* (2015) show that both offline store preference (considering an assortment interaction effect) and online store loyalty have a positive effect on online store choice. Thus, loyal customers tend to adopt multichannel offerings faster than nonloyal customers. In turn, after adopting multichannel systems, customers' overall satisfaction with and loyalty to the retailer are likely to increase even more. This mechanism is not well established though. Some studies hint at the existence of stronger attitudes when customers use multiple channels (Valentini *et al.*, 2011); however, further research is clearly required.

Customer experience has garnered a great deal of attention because consumers' purchase journeys have become more complicated as a result of the plethora of channels and touchpoints. Scholars suggest that studies should consider customer experience as a core customer outcome of multichannel retailing because it is a holistic concept and involves customers' cognitive, affective, emotional, social, and physical responses to retailers (Verhoef *et al.*, 2009). The first research question is how customer experience can be measured along the purchase journey. Second, Lemon and Verhoef (2016) present an overview on this topic and propose research directions based on different aspects, such as the drivers and consequences of customer experience, customer journey design and management, and customer experience measurement and management. We repeat their research suggestions on customer experience and call for more empirical studies. Customer experience could also be an important antecedent of customer loyalty. Thus, how can retailers improve customer experience in multichannel retailing?

8.2.2 Unresolved issues

The findings of improved satisfaction and loyalty reported in extant literature come from comparing customer perceptions of one retailer before and after implementation of a multichannel system. However, in practice, most retailers in a sector provide the same/similar multichannel systems. Thus, loyalty may decrease because (1) customers' reference level of whether they are satisfied with a retailer's service expectations increases from the overall development of multichannel retailing and (2) higher competition and price dispersion in online channels may cultivate higher price sensitivity. Although the correctness of this speculation depends on factors such as competition in a specific market and consumers' original loyal strength, we suggest that researchers explore whether a multichannel system continues to increase customer loyalty, as well as the drivers of customer loyalty to multichannel retailers.

8.2.3 Environment changes

Mobile channels have become more important in today's retail environment. A recent investigation shows that 62% of mobile users have shopped online and 42% of customers use mobile phones as their primary access to websites (Carney, 2017). However, research is still lacking on whether the use of these digital channels increases customer loyalty to retailers and which retailers specifically benefit. A similar question can be posed for other digital touchpoints, such as social media, because little is known about how these touchpoints and their interaction affect customer loyalty. Retailers also combine technologies within a specific channel; for example, they offer iPads in their offline stores or integrate social media applications (e.g., the possibility to review products and communicate with other users) on their website. Thus, the question is whether and how such technologies combined in a specific channel affect customers' channel experiences of and satisfaction with the respective retailer.

9

RQ6: Synthesized outcomes of multichannel retailing at the retailer and channel levels

In this section, we detail the impact of consumer purchase behavior in multichannel retailing on retailers and channels. A relevant substream of literature addresses how multichannel environments affect consumers' psychological cognition and, subsequently, their preferences and purchase behavior (e.g., Bhargave *et al.*, 2016; Emrich and Verhoef, 2015; Ghose and Park, 2013; Pauwels and Neslin, 2015). One explanation is that consumers' cognition affects their information processes (i.e., memory encoding, storage, and retrieval), perceptions, and experiences at all purchase stages (Puccinelli *et al.*, 2009). In an offline store having relatively rich information, for example, a reminder of the availability of online information could stimulate customer memory of the Internet and thereby enhance cognitive confidence in product information, further enhancing purchase intention (Bhargave *et al.*, 2016). Such changes of consumer cognition and intention eventually affect retailer and channel performance (e.g., sales, profit).

9.1   Retailer level

9.1.1   Channel addition and elimination

Online channel additions can lead to both advantages (e.g., extended market share, lower transaction cost) and disadvantages (e.g., consumer confusion, channel conflicts), though it is not clear which effect dominates in retailing practice. Cheng *et al.* (2007) investigate whether the addition of an online channel increases retailers' net profit by using an event study with data from the Taiwan Stock Exchange Corporation. They find that the announcement of an online channel addition directly improves investors' expectations of future cash flow and significantly increases both retailers' short-term (abnormal returns) and long-term (economic value added and market value added) performance. Homburg *et al.* (2014) use secondary data collected from the United States, Germany, and China to confirm that the announcement of a new channel positively influences retailers' stock returns. Moreover, Homburg *et al.* reveal that establishing a new channel can create more benefits in heavily competitive or turbulent markets because multiple channels help retailers resist demand fluctuations and differentiate themselves from others. However, this effect depends on retailers' predominant product category, as we discussed in RQ1. A newly added online channel for a retailer selling experience products reduces profits because of extra investments in physical stores (Ofek *et al.*, 2011).

Other studies show that adding a mobile channel to an online channel improves overall purchase amount because customers order products and services more frequently after adopting the mobile channel (Huang *et al.*, 2016; Wang *et al.*, 2015). Similarly, adding a physical store to an online or catalog store also improves retailers' total revenue, though overall returns and exchanges increase at the same time (Avery *et al.*, 2012; Pauwels and Neslin, 2015).

Retailers with multiple channels may derive benefit compensation from other channels when one channel has losses or service failures. For example, Janakiraman *et al.* (2018) discuss customers' subsequent behavior after data breach in a multichannel retailer. The authors find that customers reduce spending after their data is breached in one channel; more importantly, these customers migrate to unbreached channels of the focal retailer instead of leaving the retailer, in which case multichannel mix protects retailers from losing customers and mitigates losses in a specific channel.

The choice of channel elimination is also involved in multichannel mix and affects retail performance. Konuş *et al.* (2014) reveal a positive effect of channel elimination on retailer profits. In their field experiment, the savings from printing and mailing catalogs and also from migrating customers to the website are much larger and can offset the loss due to decreased purchase incidence after eliminating the catalog channels.

9.1.2 Multichannel shoppers

Gensler *et al.* (2012a) demonstrate that online customers have higher purchasing demands than traditional, offline-only customers, in that customers perceive greater information control, convenience, and accessibility online. However, it could also be argued that lower transaction costs online due to no traveling and waiting encourage more purchases to some extent. Moreover, studies show that online customers purchase more products and are more profitable for firms in general (Hitt and Frei, 2002; Ma, 2016). Furthermore, Li *et al.* (2015) find the late majority of adopters of an online channel are more valuable than innovators, earlier adopters, and laggards. The late majority are heavy shoppers with a high purchase frequency and volume before the online channel introduction and perceive more convenience when purchasing offline. They are loyal, have trust in retailers, and are willing to adopt the new online channel later than innovators and earlier adopters; however, they purchase less online because they remain loyal to offline channels and respond less to marketing efforts persuading them to use the online channel. Regardless, the late majority still create the highest value in all customers who adopt the website.

App adopters also tend to spend more than nonadopters (Kim *et al.*, 2015) because apps' ability to engage (through vividness, novelty, motivation, control, customization, feedback, and multiplatforming) and entertain customers increases interest in brands and products and improves purchase intention (Bellman *et al.*, 2011; Kim *et al.*, 2013).

Moreover, the net spending of app adopters can be decomposed into two competing aspects: (1) customers purchase more frequently because of apps' greater availability and convenience, and (2) customers spend less per purchase because of apps' limited screens and thus lack of ability to complete complex tasks (Huang *et al.*, 2016; Narang and Shankar, 2016).

In general, multichannel shoppers are significantly more profitable, spend more, and purchase more items across more product categories than single-channel customers (Kushwaha, 2007; Melis *et al.*, 2016; Montaguti *et al.*, 2015; Thomas and Sullivan, 2005; Venkatesan *et al.*, 2007). Multichannel customers also tend to initiate more contacts with retailers (Kumar and Venkatesan, 2005), which in turn could enhance their relationship with retailers and increase their future spending. Montaguti *et al.* (2015) suggest that multichannel shoppers are of greater value for retailers because of relatively higher satisfaction and tendency to use high-margin channels. Nevertheless, the proposition of "multichannel customers are more valuable" has boundary conditions. Kushwaha and Shankar (2013) reveal that multichannel customers (two channels versus one channel) are not necessarily the most valuable segments except for hedonic products. Cambra *et al.* (2016) replicate Kushwaha and Shankar's study in a bank service context and confirm that multichannel customers who use all the four channels are not the most profitable. The authors find that customers using some single channels as well as using specific dual-channel combinations create more value. So clearly more research is required to further understand boundary conditions, of which the industry context seems very important.

9.2 Channel level

Changes in the channel mix differently affect existing channels when adding transactional Internet-based channels. According to Dholakia *et al.* (2005), a newly added online channel does not replace an established offline channel of the same retailer. Indeed, they find that customers complete not only their original purchases but also more recent purchases in the offline channel. In general, customers' purchases from the offline channel overwhelm purchases from the online channel. Deleersnyder *et al.* (2002) confirm that the online channel addition within the newspaper industry has a small but significantly positive effect on purchase quantities of traditional newspapers. Xu *et al.* (2014) also reveal a synergy effect, such that an app addition leads to more consumption on an incumbent mobile website. However, adding an app to a website can have an opposite effect. A newly added app slightly cannibalizes both purchase frequency and amount on a website because part of the purchases are switched to the app, given that an app has significant advantages (e.g., convenience, no location and time limitation) over a website (Huang *et al.*, 2016).

In the context of adding a pure informational website to offline channels, the majority of stores in Van Nierop *et al.*'s (2011) study experienced a substantially negative impact on customer visits and spending after the channel addition. This is probably because informational websites help customers plan their purchases and easily find competitors' stores. Nevertheless, the specific effect of informational websites on offline revenues is contingent on product categories and customer segments (Pauwels *et al.*, 2011). For sensory products, which customers always evaluate through their senses (e.g., clothes, cosmetics), a synergy effect arises because the informational website complements the offline channels. This effect also exists for customers who live far away from physical stores or have high website visit frequencies.

Adding physical stores has different effects across channels as well (Avery *et al.*, 2012; Pauwels and Neslin, 2015). The addition of physical stores cannibalizes purchase frequency and sales in a retailer's catalog channel but has no effect on sales on websites or order size in catalogs and online channels. The cannibalization between stores and catalogs might be due to similar customer segments compared with the Internet, similar human capital required in the two channels, and similar amenability to experiential shopping. However, returns and exchanges in catalogs decrease because some are diverted to offline stores. Avery *et al.* (2012) also argue that in the long run, as "living" advertisements delivering rich information, physical stores strengthen customers' brand awareness; the positive customer experience and connection with retailers formed in physical stores can be transferred to established channels. Thus, newly added physical stores generate synergy effects for existing channels. Avery *et al.* show that the appearance of physical stores truly brings new customers to both websites and catalogs and encourages repeat customers to purchase in direct channels over time, thus increasing sales in these channels. Nevertheless, Wang and Goldfarb (2017) argue that when a retailer has a strong presence and is well-known locally before opening a store nearby, customers already know the information displayed in newly added stores and can easily get accustomed to the stores. In this case, new stores compete with existing websites. In the case of channel elimination, Konuş *et al.*'s (2014) show that removing the catalog channel cannibalizes the telephone channel but improves purchase incidence on websites mainly because heavy users of telephone purchasing combined with catalog searching decrease their purchases or divert to the online channel after catalog elimination.

9.3   Future research

9.3.1   Research gaps

Most studies focus on the effects of multichannel retailing on retailers' short-term performance. However, as Zhang *et al.* (2010) suggest, researchers should be careful when evaluating a multichannel retailing program using short-term results because marketing activities can have lagged effects and consumer behaviors change over time. We suggest that future research take a long-term perspective and also include other performance indicators, such as repeated purchases.

Regarding antecedents of channel performance, Melis *et al.* (2015) and Breugelmans and Campo (2016) show that in a grocery context, loyalty to a certain channel positively influences customers' purchase incidence in that channel. However, their findings do not generalize to other retailing sectors because the grocery setting differs substantially from other sectors (e.g., habitual purchases). Therefore, further knowledge on the link between channel loyalty and channel performance in other multichannel retailing sectors is required. Furthermore, little is known about the cross-channel effects of loyalty on channel performance—namely, whether and how loyalty to a certain channel influences performance of other channels of the same retailer. Further research could delve into this issue to a greater extent. Extant research also focuses on customers' past behavior and performance, but research on more forward-looking metrics, such as customer lifetime value (see Kumar and Reinartz, 2016), would be worthwhile.

As we noted previously, prior research finds that multichannel customers are generally more profitable than single-channel customers (e.g., Ansari *et al.*, 2008), thus driving companies' interests in developing multiple channels. However, little is known about the factors that affect multichannel customer profitability. For example, does the context of multichannel adoption have an impact on how profitable a customer becomes?

9.3.2 Unresolved issues

Almost all studies find that retailers' revenues and profits are improved after adding more channels. This conclusion derives from the comparison of whether the same retailer adopts a multichannel system, not from a comparison among multichannel retailers. However, the performance increment (e.g., profit, revenues) generated from a multichannel offering does not necessarily improve a focal retailer's performance in the market. Thus, the question of how retailers can improve their competitive advantage by making full use of their experience in existing channels when they step into a new channel remains. For example, as an online giant, how does Amazon use its online experience at physical stores of Whole Foods? For traditional retailers, how do they succeed with lower technological and digital capabilities?

At a channel level, cannibalization and synergy effects exist at the same time. Therefore, we propose two questions for future studies. First, should retailers allow channel cannibalization even if their total profit remains stable or increases, or is it always beneficial for retailers to resolve cannibalization? According to our synthesis, cannibalization occurs between similar channels such as mobile and online channels or physical stores and catalogs. Retailers may set large channel differentiation to alleviate channel cannibalization, which, however, may lead consumers to perceive less consistency and thus result in decreased value for retailers. Second, what is the balance between channel cannibalization and synergy?

Finally, our discussions herein should help retailers make informed decisions about allocating resources in multichannel retailing. The payoff of resource allocations differs across channels, customer segments, and marketing activities over time (Hanssens and Pauwels, 2016; Narayanan and Manchanda, 2009; Saboo *et al.*, 2016). Unfortunately, we cannot directly draw conclusions of how to allocate resources to improve retailer performance given the limited research on this topic. Thus, we call for studies to explore resource allocation with an increasing number of channels and touchpoints, especially by using big-volume data collected in various sources.

9.3.3   Environment changes

A few studies discuss the effects of newly added mobile channels on retailer performance. However, mobile websites/apps can be a separate purchase channel or an integrated technology in physical stores to facilitate customers' in-store shopping. Additional knowledge on how and when mobile websites/apps in such different contexts affect retailer performance is required. A recent study shows that 70% of retail managers are ready to adopt more advanced technologies, such as the Internet of Things, augmented reality, and virtual reality, to improve customer experiences (Columbus, 2017). Thus, further research is necessary to investigate how these types of technologies affect retailer performance. For example, how can retailers integrate new technologies that make grocery shopping more convenient (e.g., intelligent refrigerators that create retail shopping lists and automatically place an order at a focal retailer) and how is customer loyalty affected accordingly? Further research would provide valuable insights into whether investing in these new digital technologies.

10

Concluding thoughts about future retailing

The appearance of Internet-based channels prompted some people to declare the end to physical stores in retailing. More than two decades later, reports have shown that the demise of physical stores was greatly exaggerated. As Ifti Ifhar, the CEO of ComQi, a company that provides digital technologies to retailers, noted, "the real story isn't about physical retail dying. It's about evolution—and that outlook is very positive" (Ifhar, 2017). In essence, what we observe today is that retail sales in physical stores are still dominating (Howland, 2017). Moreover, retailers are integrating increasingly more technologies and touchpoints into their offline channels, while customers are continuing to visit physical stores when technology is part of the experience. According to a recent study, 75% of customers want more technology in stores, and more than 40% want it in physical stores to check prices, find items, and redeem discounts and promotions (Bouncepad, 2017). Two exemplars are Tao Cafe and Amazon Go, in which employees are not present. At Tao Cafe, customers first obtain an entrance ticket by scanning a QR code in an app before going to the store. After picking up items, customers pass through two doors: one to verify that they are leaving and the other to complete payment. At the second door, a screen shows that "products are being identified" and "products are being paid for." Payment is automatically processed through the app. At Amazon Go, the technologies of machine learning and cameras enable the store to identify the products in customers' carts and to automatically charge their store account, so customers can leave the store without taking their wallets out and waiting in a checkout line (Hartmans, 2017).

For traditional retailers, how to survive and compete with online giants will be a crucial issue. Some retailers already seem effective in these cases. Specifically, Best Buy has been able to survive in its extremely competitive and dynamic environment through a strong customer focus, while some competitors (i.e., RadioShack) have failed to do so. Best Buy even recently reported unexpected sales increases, even though it directly competes with Amazon.[1] Other store-focused retailers have a strong discount focus, such as the Dutch-based retail chain, Action, but are still showing strong sales growth.[2] The exciting environment of retail calls for further research that takes a more strategic perspective on which retail business models will survive in an increasingly digital world.

---

[1]See http://www.cnbc.com/2017/05/25/why-best-buy-shares-are-up.html.

[2]See http://www.3i.com/ /media/Files/G/Group-3i/documents/news/corporate-news/pr-action-annual-results%202015.pdf.

References

Andrews, M., J. Goehring, S. Hui, J. Pancras, and L. Thornswood (2016). "Mobile promotions: A framework and research priorities". *Journal of Interactive Marketing.* 34: 15–24.

Andrews, M., X. Luo, Z. Fang, and A. Ghose (2015). "Mobile ad effectiveness: Hyper-contextual targeting with crowdedness". *Marketing Science.* 35(2): 218–233.

Ansari, A., C. F. Mela, and S. A. Neslin (2008). "Customer channel migration". *Journal of Marketing Research.* 45(1): 60–76.

Avery, J., T. J. Steenburgh, J. Deighton, and M. Caravella (2012). "Adding bricks to clicks: Predicting the patterns of cross-channel elasticities over time". *Journal of Marketing.* 76(3): 96–111.

Baker Retailing Center (2012). *Understanding the multi-channel shopper.* Retrieved October 13, 2017 from http://www.verdegroup.com/wp-content/uploads/2012/10/The-Multi-Channel-Shopper-Market-Study.pdf.

Baker, J. (1986). "The role of the environment in marketing services: The consumer perspective. The Services Challenge: Integrating for Competitive". *Advantage.* 1(1): 79–84.

Baxendale, S., E. K. Macdonald, and H. N. Wilson (2015). "The impact of different touchpoints on brand consideration". *Journal of Retailing.* 91(2): 235–253.

Beke, F. T., F. Eggers, and P. C. Verhoef (2018). *Consumer informational privacy: Current knowledge and research directions.* forthcoming.

Bellman, S., R. F. Potter, S. Treleaven-Hassard, J. A. Robinson, and D. Varan (2011). "The effectiveness of branded mobile phone apps". *Journal of Interactive Marketing.* 25(4): 191–200.

Bendoly, E., J. D. Blocher, K. M. Bretthauer, S. Krishnan, and M. A. Venkataramanan (2005). "Online/in-store integration and customer retention". *Journal of Service Research.* 7(4): 313–327.

Berry, L. L., R. N. Bolton, C. H. Bridges, J. Meyer, A. Parasuraman, and K. Seiders (2010). "Opportunities for innovation in the delivery of interactive retail services". *Journal of Interactive Marketing.* 24(2): 155–167.

Bhargave, R., A. Mantonakis, and K. White (2016). "The cue-of-the-cloud effect: When reminders of online information availability increase purchase intentions and choice". *Journal of Marketing Research.* 53(5): 699–711.

Bilgicer, T., K. Jedidi, D. R. Lehmann, and S. A. Neslin (2015). "Social contagion and customer adoption of new sales channels". *Journal of Retailing.* 91(2): 254–271.

Bouncepad (2017). *Consumers want more tech in-store.* Retrieved June 10, 2017 from https://www.retailcustomerexperience. com/whitepapers/consumers-want-more-tech-in-store-infographic/.

Brasel, S. A. and J. Gips (2014). "Tablets, touchscreens, and touchpads: How varying touch interfaces trigger psychological ownership and endowment". *Journal of Consumer Psychology.* 24(2): 226–233.

Brasel, S. A. and J. Gips (2015). "Interface psychology: Touchscreens change attribute importance, decision criteria, and behavior in online choice". *Cyberpsychology, Behavior, and Social Networking.* 18(9): 534–538.

Breugelmans, E. and K. Campo (2016). "Cross-channel effects of price promotions: An empirical analysis of the multi-channel grocery retail sector". *Journal of Retailing.* 92(3): 333–351.

Bruner, G. C. and A. Kumar (2005). "Explaining consumer acceptance of handheld Internet devices". *Journal of Business Research.* 58(5): 553–558.

Butler, M. (2013). "Showrooming: Are retailers ready to embrace it". *The Guardian*.

Cambra, J., W. A. Kamakura, I. Melero, and F. J. Sese (2016). "Are multichannel customers really more valuable? An analysis of banking services". *International Journal of Research in Marketing*. 33(1): 208–212.

Cao, L. and L. Li (2015). "The impact of cross-channel integration on retailers' sales growth". *Journal of Retailing*. 91(2): 198–216.

Carney, D. (2017). *Shoppers moving to mobile: Where retailers fall short with m-commerce experiences*. Retrived July 24, 2017 from https://www.retailcustomerexperience.com/blogs/shoppers-moving-to-mobile-where-retailers-fall-short-with-m-commerce-experiences/?utm_source=Email_marketing&utm_campaign=emnaRCE0721 2017&cmp=1&utm_medium=html_email.

Chahal, M. (2016). *Social commerce: How willing are consumers to buy through social media?* Retrieved January 3, 2017 from https://www.marketingweek.com/2016/03/23/social-commerce-how-willing-are-consumers-to-buy-through-social-media/.

Chang, C., J. Z. Zhang, and S. Neslin (2016). *The dynamic impact of buying 'fit products' on customer learning and profitability in multichannel settings*. Retrieved from SSRN 2759679.

Chen, L. and J. Tan (2004). "Technology adaptation in E-commerce: Key determinants of virtual stores acceptance". *European Management Journal*. 22(1): 74–86.

Cheng, J. M., S. Tsao, W. Tsai, and H. H. Tu (2007). "Will eChannel additions increase the financial performance of the firm?—The evidence from Taiwan". *Industrial Marketing Management*. 36(1): 50–57.

Chiu, H., Y. Hsieh, J. Roan, K. Tseng, and J. Hsieh (2011). "The challenge for multichannel services: Cross-channel free-riding behavior". *Electronic Commerce Research and Applications*. 10(2): 268–277.

Choi, J., S. K. Hui, and D. R. Bell (2010). "Spatiotemporal analysis of imitation behavior across new buyers at an online grocery retailer". *Journal of Marketing Research*. 47(1): 75–89.

Columbus, L. (2017). *Internet of things will revolutionize retail.* Retrieved October 6, 2017 from https://www.forbes.com/sites/louis columbus/2017/03/19/internet-of-things-will-revolutionize-retail/ #2c93f5965e58.

Danaher, P. J., M. S. Smith, K. Ranasinghe, and T. S. Danaher (2015). "Where, when, and how long: Factors that influence the redemption of mobile phone coupons". *Journal of Marketing Research.* 52(5): 710–725.

Daunt, K. L. and L. C. Harris (2017). "Consumer showrooming: Value co-destruction". *Journal of Retailing and Consumer Services.* 38: 166–176.

De Haan, E., P. K. Kannan, P. C. Verhoef, and T. Wiesel (2015). *The Role of mobile devices in the online customer journey.* Working paper, Maketing Science Institute.

De Keyser, A., J. Schepers, and U. Konuş (2015). "Multichannel customer segmentation: Does the after-sales channel matter? A replication and extension". *International Journal of Research in Marketing.* 32(4): 453–456.

Degeratu, A. M., A. Rangaswamy, and J. Wu (2000). "Consumer choice behavior in online and traditional supermarkets: The effects of brand name, price, and other search attributes". *International Journal of Research in Marketing.* 17(1): 55–78.

Deleersnyder, B., I. Geyskens, K. Gielens, and M. G. Dekimpe (2002). "How cannibalistic is the internet channel? A study of the newspaper industry in the United Kingdom and the Netherlands". *International Journal of Research in Marketing.* 19(4): 337–348.

Dholakia, R. R., M. Zhao, and N. Dholakia (2005). "Multichannel retailing: A case study of early experiences". *Journal of Interactive Marketing.* 19(2): 63–74.

Dostis, M. (2016). *Victoria's secret will end catalogs, saving nearly $150M-Will no longer sell swimwear, apparel and accesssories.* Retrieved June 20, 2017 from http://www.nydailynews.com/news/ national/victoria-secret-catalogues-saving-150-million-article-1.2648817.

Dumrongsiri, A., M. Fan, A. Jain, and K. Moinzadeh (2008). "A supply chain model with direct and retail channels". *European Journal of Operational Research.* 187(3): 691–718.

Earley, A. (2017). *7 tips to combat the Amazon effect. Hint: It's the hair of the dog that bit you.* Retrieved June 17, 2017 from https://www.retailcustomerexperience.com/blogs/7-tips-to-combat-the-amazon-effect-hint-its-the-hair-of-the-dog-that-bit-you/.

Emrich, O., M. Paul, and T. Rudolph (2015). "Shopping benefits of multichannel assortment integration and the moderating role of retailer type". *Journal of Retailing.* 91(2): 326–342.

Emrich, O. and P. C. Verhoef (2015). "The impact of a homogenous versus a prototypical web design on online retail patronage for multichannel providers". *International Journal of Research in Marketing.* 32(4): 363–374.

Episerver (2015). *Multichannel digital marketing report 2015.* Retrieved October 13, 2017 from http://www.episerver.com/learn/resources/research–reports/multichannel-digital-marketing-report-2015/.

Falk, T., J. Schepers, M. Hammerschmidt, and H. H. Bauer (2007). "Identifying cross-channel dissynergies for multichannel service providers". *Journal of Service Research.* 10(2): 143–160.

Fong, N. M., Z. Fang, and X. Luo (2015). "Geo-conquesting: Competitive locational targeting of mobile promotions". *Journal of Marketing Research.* 52(5): 726–735.

Frambach, R. T., H. C. Roest, and T. V. Krishnan (2007). "The impact of consumer internet experience on channel preference and usage intentions across the different stages of the buying process". *Journal of Interactive Marketing.* 21(2): 26–41.

Friedman, L. G. and T. R. Furey (2003). *The channel advantage.* Burlington, MA: Butterworth-Heinemann.

Fritz, W., S. Sohn, and B. Seegebarth (2017). "Broadening the perspective on mobile marketing: An introduction". *Psychology & Marketing.* 34(2): 113–118.

Gallino, S., A. Moreno, and I. Stamatopoulos (2016). *Channel integration, sales dispersion, and inventory management. Management Science.* Retrieved October 13, 2017 from http://doi.org/10/1287/mnsc.2016.2479.

Gao, F. and X. Su (2017). "Omnichannel retail operations with buy-online-and-pick-up-in-store". *Management Science.* 63(8): 2478–2492.

Gensler, S., P. S. Leeflang, and B. Skiera (2012a). "Impact of online channel use on customer revenues and costs to serve: Considering product portfolios and self-selection". *International Journal of Research in Marketing.* 29(2): 192–201.

Gensler, S., S. A. Neslin, and P. C. Verhoef (2017). "The showrooming phenomenon: It's more than just about price". *Journal of Interactive Marketing.* 38: 29–43.

Gensler, S., P. C. Verhoef, and M. Böhm (2012b). "Understanding consumers' multichannel choices across the different stages of the buying process". *Marketing Letters.* 23(4): 987–1003.

Geyskens, I., K. Gielens, and M. G. Dekimpe (2002). "The market valuation of internet channel additions". *Journal of Marketing.* 66(2): 102–119.

Ghaleno, M. R., M. R. Zavareh, and E. Bahrami (2016). "Effect of mobile marketing on customer-oriented brand equity in insurance industry". *International Journal of Management, Accounting and Economics.* 3(3): 185–201.

Ghose, A. and S. H. Park (2013). *The negative impact of mobile devices on niche product consumption. in paper read at Thirty Fourth Internet Different Conference on Information Systems.*

Grewal, D., K. L. Ailawadi, D. Gauri, K. Hall, P. Kopalle, and J. R. Robertson (2011). "Innovations in retail pricing and promotions". *Journal of Retailing.* 87: S43–S52.

Grewal, D. and M. Levy (2007). "Retailing research: Past, present, and future". *Journal of Retailing.* 83(4): 447–464.

Gu, R., L. Oh, and K. Wang (2013). "Differential impact of web and mobile interactivity on e-retailers' performance". *Journal of Organizational Computing and Electronic Commerce.* 23(4): 325–349.

Ha, S. and L. Stoel (2009). "Consumer e-shopping acceptance: Antecedents in a technology acceptance model". *Journal of Business Research.* 62(5): 565–571.

Hanssens, D. M. and K. H. Pauwels (2016). "Demonstrating the value of marketing". *Journal of Marketing.* 80(6): 173–190.

Hartmans, A. (2017). *Technical issues are forcing Amazon to delay the public launch of its cashier-less grocery store.* Retrieved June 2, 2017 from http://www.businessinsider.com/amazon-go-grocery-store-opening-delayed-due-to-technical-issues-2017-3?international=true&r=US&IR=T.

Herhausen, D., J. Binder, M. Schoegel, and A. Herrmann (2015). "Integrating bricks with clicks: Retailer-level and channel-level outcomes of online–offline channel integration". *Journal of Retailing.* 91(2): 309–325.

Hitt, L. M. and F. X. Frei (2002). "Do better customers utilize electronic distribution channels? The case of PC banking". *Management Science.* 48(6): 732–748.

Hoch, D. (2014). *App retention improves-apps used only once declines to 20%.* Retrieved January 28, 2017 from http://info.localytics.com/blog/app-retention-improves.

Homburg, C., J. Vollmayr, and A. Hahn (2014). "Firm value creation through major channel expansions: Evidence from an event study in the United States, Germany, and China". *Journal of Marketing.* 78(3): 38–61.

Howland, D. (2017). *Study: Amazon dominated online, but physical stores still retain the advantage.* Retrieved June 25, 2017 from http://www.retaildive.com/news/study-amazon-dominates-online-but-physical-stores-retain-the-advantage/445507/.

Huang, L., X. Lu, and S. Ba (2016). "An empirical study of the cross-channel effects between web and mobile shopping channels". *Information & Management.* 53(2): 265–278.

Hubert, M., M. Blut, C. Brock, C. Backhaus, and T. Eberhardt (2017). "Acceptance of Smartphone – based mobile shopping: Mobile benefits, customer characteristics, perceived risks, and the impact of application context". *Psychology & Marketing.* 34(2): 175–194.

Ifhar, I. (2017). *The demise of brick-and-mortar retail has been greatly ex-aggerated*. Retrieved July 15, 2017 from https://www.retailcustomer experience.com/blogs/the-demise-of-bricks-and-mortar-retail-has-been-greatly-exaggerated-2/?utm_source=Email_marketing&utm_campaign=emnaRCE07122017121505&cmp=1&utm_medium=HTMLEmail.

Inman, J. J., V. Shankar, and R. Ferraro (2004). "The roles of channel-category associations and geodemographics in channel patronage". *Journal of Marketing*. 68(2): 51–71.

Janakiraman, R., J. H. Lim, and R. Rishika (2018). "The effect of a data breach announcement on customer behavior: Evidence from a multichannel retailer". *Journal of Marketing*. 82(2): 85–105.

Jindal, R. P., W. J. Reinartz, M. Krafft, and W. D. Hoyer (2007). "Determinants of the variety of routes to market". *International Journal of Research in Marketing*. 24(1): 17–29.

Joo, M., K. C. Wilbur, B. Cowgill, and Y. Zhu (2014). "Television advertising and online search". *Management Science*. 60(1): 56–73.

Kim, E., J. S. Lin, and Y. Sung (2013). "To app or not to app: Engaging consumers via braned mobile apps". *Journal of Interactive Advertising*. 13(1): 53–65.

Kim, S. J., R. J. Wang, and E. C. Malthouse (2015). "The effects of adopting and using a brand's mobile application on customers' subsequent purchase behavior". *Journal of Interactive Marketing*. 31: 28–41.

Ko, E., E. Y. Kim, and E. K. Lee (2009). "Modeling consumer adoption of mobile shopping for fashion products in Korea". *Psychology & Marketing*. 26(7): 669–687.

Kollmann, T., A. Kuckertz, and I. Kayser (2012). "Cannibalization or synergy? Consumers' channel selection in online–offline multichannel systems". *Journal of Retailing and Consumer Services*. 19(2): 186–194.

Konuş, U., S. A. Neslin, and P. C. Verhoef (2014). "The effect of search channel elimination on purchase incidence, order size and channel choice". *International Journal of Research in Marketing*. 31(1): 49–64.

Konuş, U., P. C. Verhoef, and S. A. Neslin (2008). "Multichannel shopper segments and their covariates". *Journal of Retailing*. 84(4): 398–413.

Kumar, V. (2010). "A customer lifetime value-based approach to marketing in the multichannel, multimedia retailing environment". *Journal of Interactive Marketing*. 24(20): 71–85.

Kumar, V. and W. J. Reinartz (2016). "Creating enduring customer value". *Journal of Marketing*. 80(6): 36–68.

Kumar, V. and R. Venkatesan (2005). "Who are the multichannel shoppers and how do they perform?: Correlates of multichannel shopping behavior". *Journal of Interactive Marketing*. 19(2): 44–62.

Kushwaha, T. L. (2007). "Essays on Multichannel Marketing. Doctoral dissertation, Texas A&M University".

Kushwaha, T. L. and V. Shankar (2013). "Are multichannel customers really more valuable? The moderating role of product category characteristics". *Journal of Marketing*. 77(4): 67–85.

Lemon, K. N. and P. C. Verhoef (2016). "Understanding customer experience throughout the customer journey". *Journal of Marketing*. 80(6): 69–96.

Levy, M. and B. A. Weitz (2009). *Retailing management*. New York: The McGraw-Hills/Irwin companies.

Lewis, J., P. Whysall, and C. Foster (2014). "Drivers and technology-related obstacles in moving to multichannel retailing". *International Journal of Electronic Commerce*. 18(4): 43–68.

Li, B. and F. Tang (2011). "Online pricing dynamics in internet retailing: The case of the DVD market". *Electronic Commerce Research and Applications*. 10(2): 227–236.

Li, C., X. Luo, C. Zhang, and X. Wang (2017). "Sunny, rainy, and cloudy with a chance of mobile promotion effectiveness". *Marketing Science*. 36(5): 762–779.

Li, J., U. Konuş, K. Pauwels, and F. Langerak (2015). "The hare and the tortoise: Do earlier adopters of online channels purchase more?" *Journal of Retailing*. 91(2): 289–308.

Liangyu (2017). *China foucus: Alibaba's self-service TaoCafe takes e-shopping offline*. Retrieved July 16, 2017 from http://news.xin huanet.com/english/2017-07/11/c_136434967.htm.

Lin, H. (2012). "The effect of multi-channel service quality on mobile customer loyalty in an online-and-mobile retail context". *The Service Industries Journal*. 32(11): 1865–1882.

Lin, J. C. and H. Lu (2000). "Towards an understanding of the behavioural intention to use a web site". *International Journal of Information Management*. 20(3): 197–208.

Lobschat, L., E. C. Osinga, and W. J. Reinartz (2017). "What happens online stays offline? Segment-specific online and offline effects of banner advertisements". *Journal of Marketing Research*. 54(6): 901–913.

Lund, D. J. and D. Marinova (2014). "Managing revenue across retail channels: The interplay of service performance and direct marketing". *Journal of Marketing*. 78(5): 99–118.

Lusch, R. F. and S. L. Vargo (2011). "Service-dominant logic: A necessary step". *European Journal of Marketing*. 45(7/8): 1289–1309.

Lynch Jr, J. G. and D. Ariely (2000). "Wine online: Search costs affect competition on price, quality, and distribution". *Marketing Science*. 19(1): 83–103.

Ma, J. (2016). "Does greater online assortment pay? An empirical study using matched online and catalog shoppers". *Journal of Retailing*. 92(3): 373–382.

McGoldrick, P. J. and N. Collins (2007). "Multichannel retailing: Profiling the multichannel shopper". *International Review of Retail, Distribution and Consumer Research*. 17(2): 139–158.

Melero, I., F. J. Sese, and P. C. Verhoef (2016). "Recasting the customer experience in today's omni-channel environment 1/Redefiniendo la experiencia del cliente en el entorno omnicanal". *Universia Business Review*. 50: 18.

Melis, K., K. Campo, E. Breugelmans, and L. Lamey (2015). "The impact of the multi-channel retail mix on online store choice: Does online experience matter?" *Journal of Retailing*. 91(2): 272–288.

Melis, K., K. Campo, L. Lamey, and E. Breugelmans (2016). "A bigger slice of the multichannel grocery pie: When does consumers' online channel use expand retailers' share of wallet?" *Journal of Retailing*. 92(3): 268–286.

Mindtree (2015). *Winning today's global phy-gital shoppers.* Retrieved October 13, 2017 from https://www.mindtree.com/phygitalshopper/global/pdf/mindtree-global-detailed-report.pdf.

Montaguti, E., S. A. Neslin, and S. Valentini (2015). "Can marketing campaigns induce multichannel buying and more profitable customers? A field experiment". *Marketing Science.* 35(2): 201–217.

Montoya-Weiss, M. M., G. B. Voss, and D. Grewal (2003). "Determinants of online channel use and overall satisfaction with a relational, multichannel service provider". *Journal of the Academy of Marketing Science.* 31(4): 448–458.

Morrison, K. (2015). *91% of retail brands use two or more social media channels.* Retrieved December 20, 2016 from http://www.adweek.com/digital/yesmail-retail-brands-social-media-channels/.

Naik, P. A. and K. Peters (2009). "A hierarchical marketing communications model of online and offline media synergies". *Journal of Interactive Marketing.* 23(4): 288–299.

Narang, U. and V. Shankar (2016). *The effects of mobile apps on shopper purchases and product returns.* Retrieved from SSRN: https://ssrn.com/abstract=2878903 or http://dx.doi.org/10.2139/ssrn.2878903.

Narayanan, S. and P. Manchanda (2009). "Heterogeneous learning and the targeting of marketing communication for new products". *Marketing Science.* 28(3): 424–441.

Neslin, S. A., D. Grewal, R. Leghorn, V. Shankar, M. L. Teerling, J. S. Thomas, and P. C. Verhoef (2006). "Challenges and opportunities in multichannel customer management". *Journal of Service Research.* 9(2): 95–112.

Neslin, S. A. and V. Shankar (2009). "Key issues in multichannel customer management: Current knowledge and future directions". *Journal of Interactive Marketing.* 23(1): 70–81.

Nicholson, M., I. Clarke, and M. Blakemore (2002). "'One brand, three ways to shop': Situational variables and multichannel consumer behaviour". *The International Review of Retail, Distribution and Consumer Research.* 12(2): 131–148.

Noble, S. M., D. A. Griffith, and M. G. Weinberger (2005). "Consumer derived utilitarian value and channel utilization in a multi-channel retail context". *Journal of Business Research*. 58(12): 1643–1651.

O'Cass, A. and T. Fenech (2003). "Web retailing adoption: Exploring the nature of internet users web retailing behaviour". *Journal of Retailing and Consumer Services*. 10(2): 81–94.

Ofek, E., Z. Katona, and M. Sarvary (2011). "'Bricks and clicks': The impact of product returns on the strategies of multichannel retailers". *Marketing Science*. 30(1): 42–60.

Olbrich, R. and C. D. Schultz (2014). "Multichannel advertising: Does print advertising affect search engine advertising?" *European Journal of Marketing*. 48(9/10): 1731–1756.

Pauwels, K., P. S. Leeflang, M. L. Teerling, and K. E. Huizingh (2011). "Does online information drive offline revenues?: Only for specific products and consumer segments!" *Journal of Retailing*. 87(1): 1–17.

Pauwels, K. and S. A. Neslin (2015). "Building with bricks and mortar: The revenue impact of opening physical stores in a multichannel environment". *Journal of Retailing*. 91(2): 182–197.

Phillips, C. (2013). *'Webrooming' – new trend holds promise for in-store sales*. Retrieved February 27, 2017 from http://www.powerretail.com.au/multichannel/accenture-seamless-retail-study/.

Polo, Y. and F. J. Sese (2016). "Does the nature of the interaction matter? Understanding customer channel choice for purchases and communications". *Journal of Service Research*. 19(2): 276–290.

Prins, R., P. C. Verhoef, and P. H. Franses (2009). "The impact of adoption timing on new service usage and early disadoption". *International Journal of Research in Marketing*. 26(4): 304–313.

Puccinelli, N. M., R. C. Goodstein, D. Grewal, and R. Price (2009). "Customer experience management in retailing: Understanding the buying process". *Journal of Retailing*. 85(1): 15–30.

Rangaswamy, A. and G. H. Van Bruggen (2005). "Opportunities and challenges in multichannel marketing: An introduction to the special issue". *Journal of Interactive Marketing*. 19(2): 5–11.

Ratchford, B. T. (2009). "Online pricing: Review and directions for research". *Journal of Interactive Marketing*. 23(1): 82–90.

Retail Customer Experience (2016). *Amazon Go promises no check-out, no Lines, no waiting.* Retrieved March 5, 2017 from https://www.retailcustomerexperience.com/news/amazon-go-promises-no-checkout-no-lines-no-waiting/.

Retail Customer Experience (2017). *Walmart rolls out pickup kiosks in Arizona, Oklahoma, Alabama, Georgia and Virginia.* Retrieved July 10, 2017 from https://www.retailcustomerexperience.com/news/walmart-rolls-out-pickup-kiosks-in-arizona-oklahoma-alabama-georgia-and-virginia/.

Rust, R. T. and M. Huang (2012). "Optimizing service productivity". *Journal of Marketing.* 76(2): 47–66.

Saboo, A. R., V. Kumar, and I. Park (2016). "Using big data to model time-varying effects for marketing resource (re) allocation". *MIS Quarterly.* 40(4): 911–939.

Schiff, J. L. (2015). *8 ways to create a successful multichannel customer experience.* Retrieved November 28, 2016 from http://www.cio.com/article/2887285/e-commerce/8-ways-to-create-a-successful-multichannel-customer-experience.html.

Schoenbachler, D. D. and G. L. Gordon (2002). "Multi-channel shopping: Understanding what drives channel choice". *Journal of Consumer Marketing.* 19(1): 42–53.

Schröder, H. and S. Zaharia (2008). "Linking multi-channel customer behavior with shopping motives: An empirical investigation of a German retailer". *Journal of Retailing and Consumer Services.* 15(6): 452–468.

Shankar, V. and S. Balasubramanian (2009). "Mobile marketing: A synthesis and prognosis". *Journal of Interactive Marketing.* 23(2): 118–129.

Shankar, V., A. K. Smith, and A. Rangaswamy (2003). "Customer satisfaction and loyalty in online and offline environments". *International Journal of Research in Marketing.* 20(2): 153–175.

Shen, G. C., J. Chiou, C. Hsiao, C. Wang, and H. Li (2016). "Effective marketing communication via social networking site: The moderating role of the social tie". *Journal of Business Research.* 69(6): 2265–2270.

Shim, S., M. A. Eastlick, S. L. Lotz, and P. Warrington (2001). "An online prepurchase intentions model: The role of intention to search". *Journal of Retailing*. 77(3): 397–416.

SmartBear (2014). *2014 state of mobile*. Retrieved December 22, 2016 from https://smartbear.com/news/news-releases/the-state-of-mobile-testing-2014/.

Sopadjieva, E., U. M. Dholakia, and B. Benjamin (2017). *A study of 46,000 shoppers shows that omnichannel retailing works*. Retrieved January 20, 2017 from https://hbr.org/2017/01/a-study-of-46000-shoppers-shows-that-omnichannel-retailing-works.

Sousa, R. and C. A. Voss (2006). "Service quality in multichannel services employing virtual channels". *Journal of Service Research*. 8(4): 356–371.

Sultan, F., A. J. Rohm, and T. T. Gao (2009). "Factors influencing consumer acceptance of mobile marketing: A two-country study of youth markets". *Journal of Interactive Marketing*. 23(4): 308–320.

Teerling, M. L. and E. K. Huizingh (2005). *The complementarity between online and offline consumer attitudes and behavior*. Working paper: University of Groningen, the Netherlands.

Thomas, J. S. and U. Y. Sullivan (2005). "Managing marketing communications with multichannel customers". *Journal of Marketing*. 69(4): 239–251.

Valentini, S., E. Montaguti, and S. A. Neslin (2011). "Decision process evolution in customer channel choice". *Journal of Marketing*. 75(6): 72–86.

Van Baal, S. and C. Dach (2005). "Free riding and customer retention across retailers' channels". *Journal of Interactive Marketing*. 19(2): 75–85.

Van Birgelen, M., A. De Jong, and K. De Ruyter (2006). "Multi-channel service retailing: The effects of channel performance satisfaction on behavioral intentions". *Journal of Retailing*. 82(4): 367–377.

Van Doorn, J. and J. C. Hoekstra (2013). "Customization of online advertising: The role of intrusiveness". *Marketing Letters*. 24(4): 339–351.

Van Nierop, J. E. M., P. S. Leeflang, M. L. Teerling, and K. E. Huizingh (2011). "The impact of the introduction and use of an informational website on offline customer buying behavior". *International Journal of Research in Marketing*. 28(2): 155–165.

Venkatesan, R., V. Kumar, and N. Ravishanker (2007). "Multichannel shopping: Causes and consequences". *Journal of Marketing*. 71(2): 114–132.

Verhoef, P. C. (2012). "Multichannel customer management strategy". In: *Handbook of marketing strategy*. Ed. by V. Shankar and G. Garpenter. Cheltenham: Edward Elgar Publishing Limited. 135–150.

Verhoef, P. C. and B. Donkers (2005). "The effect of acquisition channels on customer loyalty and cross-Buying". *Journal of Interactive Marketing*. 19(2): 31–43.

Verhoef, P. C., P. K. Kannan, and J. J. Inman (2015). "From multi-channel retailing to omni-channel retailing: Introduction to the special issue on multi-channel retailing". *Journal of Retailing*. 91(2): 174–181.

Verhoef, P. C. and F. Langerak (2001). "Possible determinants of consumers' adoption of electronic grocery shopping in the Netherlands". *Journal of Retailing and Consumer Services*. 8(5): 275–285.

Verhoef, P. C., K. N. Lemon, A. Parasuraman, A. Roggeveen, M. Tsiros, and L. A. Schlesinger (2009). "Customer experience creation: Determinants, dynamics and management strategies". *Journal of Retailing*. 85(1): 31–41.

Verhoef, P. C., S. A. Neslin, and B. Vroomen (2007). "Multichannel customer management: Understanding the research-shopper phenomenon". *International Journal of Research in Marketing*. 24(2): 129–148.

Verhoef, P. C., A. T. Stephen, P. K. Kannan, X. Luo, V. Abhishek, and M. Andrews (2017). "Consumer connectivity in a complex, technology-enabled, and mobile-oriented world with smart products". *Journal of Interactive Marketing*. 40: 1–8.

Vijayasarathy, L. R. (2004). "Predicting consumer intentions to use on-line shopping: The case for an augmented technology acceptance model". *Information & Management.* 41(6): 747–762.

Voorveld, H. A., E. G. Smit, P. C. Neijens, and A. F. Bronner (2016). "Consumers' cross-channel use in online and offline purchases". *Journal of Advertising Research.* 56(4): 385–400.

Wallace, D. W., J. L. Giese, and J. L. Johnson (2004). "Customer retailer loyalty in the context of multiple channel strategies". *Journal of Retailing.* 80(4): 249–263.

Wang, K. and A. Goldfarb (2017). "Can offline stores drive online sales?" *Journal of Marketing Research.* 54(5): 706–719.

Wang, R. J., E. C. Malthouse, and L. Krishnamurthi (2015). "On the go: How mobile shopping affects customer purchase behavior". *Journal of Retailing.* 91(2): 217–234.

Wang, X., C. Yu, and Y. Wei (2012). "Social media peer communication and impacts on purchase intentions: A consumer socialization framework". *Journal of Interactive Marketing.* 26(4): 198–208.

Wilson, H., R. Street, and L. Bruce (2008). *The Multichannel Challenge.* Routledge.

Wolk, A. and C. Ebling (2010). "Multi-channel price differentiation: An empirical investigation of existence and causes". *International Journal of Research in Marketing.* 27(2): 142–150.

Wolny, J. and N. Charoensuksai (2016). "Multichannel customer journeys: Mapping the effects of zmot, showrooming and webrooming". In: *Marketing Challenges in a Turbulent Business Environment.* Ed. by M. Groza and C. Ragland. 205–206.

Xu, J., C. Forman, J. B. Kim, and K. Van Ittersum (2014). "News media channels: Complements or substitutes? Evidence from mobile phone usage". *Journal of Marketing.* 78(4): 97–112.

Xue, M., L. M. Hitt, and P. Chen (2011). "Determinants and outcomes of internet banking adoption". *Management Science.* 57(2): 291–307.

Zhang, J., P. W. Farris, J. W. Irvin, T. Kushwaha, T. J. Steenburgh, and B. A. Weitz (2010). "Crafting integrated multichannel retailing strategies". *Journal of Interactive Marketing.* 24(2): 168–180.

Zhang, J. and M. Wedel (2009). "The effectiveness of customized promotions in online and offline stores". *Journal of Marketing Research*. 46(2): 190–206.

Zhang, X. (2009). "Retailers' multichannel and price advertising strategies". *Marketing Science*. 28(6): 1080–1094.